SOLVING
CONFLICTS

SOLVING CONFLICTS

A Peace Research Perspective

JOHAN GALTUNG

University of Hawaii Institute for Peace

Honolulu

Library of Congress Cataloging-in-Publication Data

Galtung, Johan.
    Solving conflicts : a peace research perspective / Johan Galtung.
      p.   cm.
    Bibliography: p.
    ISBN 0-8248-1263-8
    1. International relations. 2. Peace. I. University of Hawaii
at Manoa. Institute for Peace. II. Title.
JK1391.G27   1989
327'.09'048—dc20   89-5049
                                                    CIP

Distributed by
University of Hawaii Press
Order Department
2840 Kolowalu Street
Honolulu, Hawaii 96822

CONTENTS

Preface   vii

CHAPTER 1
The ''East-West'' Conflict   1

CHAPTER 2
The ''North-South'' Conflict   21

CHAPTER 3
The ''Middle East'' Conflict   37

Notes   59

PREFACE

The University of Hawaii Institute for Peace asked me to give three public lectures during the spring term of 1988 on conflict resolution, focusing on the conflicts most often mentioned in the United States —"East-West," "North-South," and the "Middle East." The lectures are offered here in a more permanent form, but essentially as originally presented. A few minor revisions have been made and notes have been added.

I would like to express my gratitude to the UHIP for inviting me to give the lectures, to the participants in the symposia for their excellent comments, to Jon van Dyke and George Simson for their helpful advice, and to Carolyn DiPalma for a superb job preparing the manuscript.

CHAPTER 1

The "East-West" Conflict

There is a complication already from the beginning: "East-West" conflict, in quotation marks. Why? Because the conflict is mainly between the world *north*east and *north*west, with some of the world *southeast*. It is a conflict predominantly in the Northern Hemisphere, between the First and the Second worlds, with a solid core conflict between the two superpowers, the United States and the Soviet Union. And it has an even more solid core inside those two countries in terms of relatively entrenched elites with particular values and interests. Let us not bestow too much dignity on it by pretending the whole world is involved. Most of the world is watching, often in disbelief.[1] The Third World tends to see the arms race as a waste, to be converted into development.

That said, let us now try to get at the problem, and see where we stand on the possibility of solving the conflict. Let me begin by distancing myself from the idea that the INF agreement of December 8, 1987 represents a solution to the East-West conflict. I should like to point out eight of the key shortcomings.

First, the agreement concerns only land-based missiles (not the sea-launched and air-launched types). They are now being deployed, not under the usual slogan of "modernization," but under the additional slogan of "compensation." In essence the agreement can be seen as a triumph of the United States Air Force and Navy over the Army.

Second, the agreement concerns only the land-based missiles owned by the United States, the Soviet Union, and Germany, not those owned by France.

Third, the agreement concerns only the intermediate-range missiles with a range of from about 300 to 3,000 miles (500 to 5,000 kilometers), meaning that work is now on the way to modernize missiles

1

below the 300-mile range, and possibly also have more of them above 3,000 miles, again to "compensate."

Fourth, the agreement concerns only the missiles (they are to be scrapped in a quite imaginative way), not the warheads, which are to be saved in order, for instance, to be put into sea-launched and air-launched missiles (SLCMs and ALCMs) by Washington and London, and possibly also by Moscow.

Fifth, the agreement concerns only nuclear capabilities, and not, for instance, chemical arms that were being produced by the United States again, after a moratorium of eighteen years.

Sixth, the agreement does not broach the key issue: the possible offensive use of "Star Wars" technologies, by using ground-based generators for lasers reflected from outer space by geo-stationary mirrors. This is the essence of the experiments launched in 1988 on Maui, in the Hawaiian archipelago, using the University of Hawaii observatory at the top of Haleakala, and AVCO (private, under Air Force contract).[2]

Seventh, the agreement offers nothing new in the basic underlying issue that is almost never touched, the script driving it all: military doctrine. There is no reflection in U.S. media reports of the basic shift in thinking now taking place in so many European countries, including the Soviet Union, away from offensive doctrines based on retaliation and toward defensive, nonprovocative doctrines based on defensive deterrence; "sufficient defense" in Gorbachev's language. That discourse is as closed as ever in the United States.[3]

Eighth, the agreement does not reflect any constructive thinking in the field of positive peace, of building new ties between the superpowers or the parties in general, or healing the wounds in the old continent of Europe, for instance those of Germany/Berlin.

In other words, if this is an approach to peace, then it is still very, very much peace with warlike means, not the peace with peaceful means that the peace movement is longing for and the peace research movement explores. And yet the INF was significant, and in a major way. As an arms control agreement it is very seriously flawed. As an indicator that the Cold War is over it carries very good portents indeed.

I shall now dig into this quite intractable problem. To do so I have to introduce a bit of conflict resolution theory, and in order to develop that we need a minimal amount of conflict theory. And for a minimum of conflict theory I would suggest three letters: *A, B* and

C. A stands for attitude, *B* stands for behavior, and *C* stands for conflict.

A stands for the attitudinal aspect of conflict and can be divided into two parts: cognitive and emotive. The most important aspect of the cognitive part is the construction of what the Germans call a *Feindbild,* the image of the enemy, and what in a much more useful American expression is called Self-Other images. The Department of Political Science at the University of Hawaii stands a fair chance of becoming a world leader when it comes to elaborating that particular theme. The Self-Other image has built into it a very important aspect: what matters is not only how you conceive of Other, but also how you conceive of your Self. It is the difference, or gradient, between the two images that matters. At that point the emotive aspect enters fully; how can you avoid loving Self when you have such an inflated image, and how can you help hating the enemy Other when he simply is a-human, antihuman, subhuman?

B stands for the behavioral aspects of conflict. One of the many such aspects uses the attitudes as point of departure, builds on them and crystallizes them into patterns of behavioral polarization. The cognitive and the emotive aspects of the attitudinal dimension have already prepared for the crystallization of the images. There is polarization in the mind; the world is readily divided into black and white. And that polarization is then enacted with positive relations within the alliance, and low-level, or negative, contact between alliances. If there is real contact, then only in a regulated manner between the superpowers, and, more particularly, between the super-leaders of the superpowers and even more dramatically as a summit meeting. A summit meeting is a symptom of the pathology of the system. A summit meeting is not to be celebrated, rather it is to be seen as a conflict manifestation, essentially for reasons I am coming to later. It may be effective in the course of waging a war as shown by the meetings of the Allied leaders in the Second World War, but hardly in waging peace.

The second aspect of *B* for behavior is then, of course, readiness for destructive action, not to mention destructive action itself. If Self and Other are anything like what the attitudinal aspect has prepared people to believe, then one will certainly need to do something about it. If Self = God and Other = Devil, then one had better protect God and be prepared to fight the Devil. The consequence of this is an arms race, and even an escalating arms race. For the ultimate enemy, one needs the ultimate weapons, those of mass destruction. Ultimate weapons lead to ultimate strategies built on extermination (or the threat of extermination). The best alliance doctrine becomes a problem of jockeying for the best initial position should a war begin.

Attitude and behavior reinforce each other; that is easy enough. But conflict analysis does not stop with A and B. Attitude and behavior are only preliminaries. It is with C that real conflict analysis starts. C stands for conflict, and conflict means incompatibility of goals, of one or more actors or parties. It means that what one actor tries to do stands in the way of what another actor tries to do; that the values of one actor stand in the way of another; and that the interests of one party stand in the way of another.

Dividing goals in this way into values and interests is rather fundamental in conflict theory. Just as I said that there are two basic types of attitudes and two basic types of behavior, I am now saying there are two basic types of conflict. Conflict over clearly articulated values between conscious, strategy-planning actors is one thing; conflict between parties over interests embedded in social structure—parties that do not even, in a sense, know what is going on—is quite another. It is not only those at the bottom that are unconscious of what is going on; the party at the top is also often unable to explain the origin of its own power and privilege. In the East-West conflict we are definitely not dealing with that second type of conflict—we are dealing with the first type. We have heavily crystallized actors. They know quite well what their goals are. They have strategies to pursue them. In other words, we are in conflict of type I, what the conflict analyst might call direct conflict. Conflict of type II is structural conflict; that is what the North-South conflict, to a large extent, is about. For that reason the theory of the North-South conflict becomes much more complex. And the theory of the Middle East conflict combines both aspects. But my point of departure right now is that we are dealing with conflict of type I; and we should proceed accordingly, having diagnosed the phenomenon.

In addition to A, B, and C there is a further distinction—that between the intra-approach and the inter-approach to conflicts. Let me start with the inter-approach, which sees the conflict as located between two or more actors or parties. Conflict becomes an exchange of hostile behavior, grounded in mutually hostile attitudes, over some issue. That issue is what the conflict is about. This approach is important and indispensable in any conflict analysis.

But equally important and indispensable is the intra-approach. We then look at both actors separately and ask: What could it be inside these actors that might generate a conflict, that might fashion their attitudes and behavior and make them more or less suitable for conflict resolution? This approach is often favored by people to the left politically, who believe that inter-actor conflict comes out of intra-actor characteristics, such as a capitalist structure in search of markets and raw materials. Conversely, the inter-approach is often preferred by people to the right who do not see the need for any basic intra-change, but are eager to bring the parties together, trying to get the system running again.

As you can guess, if I have three aspects of conflict on the one hand —*A, B,* and *C*—and then intra and inter on the other, it is inevitable that I should end up with a 3 × 2 table with six combinations. In any approach to conflict there are six aspects to explore: the intra and the inter, the within and between aspects, of attitudes, behavior, and conflict. If we want to solve the East-West conflict we have to look at all of them. No reductionism is good enough, neither of the leftist nor of the rightist varieties.

Let me make use of this to point out how utterly naive it is to believe that we can solve the East-West conflict by approaching only the behavioral aspects, and only the military part of them; moreover, as if it is only a conflict between two countries. One way of doing this is precisely by having only the superpowers come together at the top level, at a summit meeting. Persons believing that this is the solution to the conflict are themselves victims of the conflict. That victimized state is one of the key factors maintaining the conflict system, and it had, in December 1987, an apogee in the United States of America, supported by individual-oriented, structure-blind, practically speaking knowledge-free media.[4]

Let me now give an image of what I mean by conflict resolution. Let us suppose two parties are faced with a real incompatibility. A solution is proposed. But is the solution fair? Is it objective? Is it stable, is it lasting, does it stick? I want that piece of land. You also want that piece of land. The incompatibility looms high on the horizon. There is a very solid behavioral pattern of polarization, and heavy build-up of destructive machineries. There is the attitudinal build-up, both in terms of a cognitive map and an emotive distribution across the cognitive map, combining Self-love with Other-hatred. The situation begins to look serious. Conflict resolution, meaning efforts to trace a trajectory from *A, B, C* to non-*A*, non-*B*, non-*C* looks forbidding. And we are not going to fool ourselves by believing it is enough if we resolve only one of them.

Thus, non-*A* means a correction of steep Self-Other gradients on both sides. Non-*B* means a correction of polarization patterns and destruction machinery. Non-*C* means that the incompatibilities are either removed or that the goals and interests associated with them are receding into the background. If conflict is actors in pursuit of incompatible goals, then there are several ways of solving a conflict. We can remove the incompatibility. But we can also remove the pursuit if one or more of the actors simply says: "I am not interested in it any longer. It does not mean that much to me. I am willing to go for one half, to compromise." There are several ways of getting to that point. I will not display the whole array of possibilities. The important point is not to "solve" conflicts by getting rid of the actors themselves, by having them destroy each other, or being destroyed by a third party out to maintain "law and order." The goal is an outcome accepted by the parties involved.

To arrive at an image of East-West conflict resolution it might be useful to look at *A, B,* and *C* separately, and then try to look at the trajectories I mentioned.

So maybe we should start, in counter-alphabetical order, with the conflict itself. This brings us to a question to which not many people have a ready answer: Do you remember what the East-West conflict was about? It was not about hatred. And it was not about arms build-up. It was about something totally different. More particularly, I think it was essentially about American/Soviet incompatibilities and in a quite specific manner. One of them was over values, and the other was over interests. More precisely, it reads something like this: There is one party called West, with a center of gravity in the United States after the Second World War, totally convinced that the world would be a better place if the culture of liberalism/conservatism and the structures of capitalism and democracy were distributed all over the world. Then there is another party called East, with a center of gravity in the Soviet Union after the Second World War, equally convinced that the values indicated by the words marxism/socialism should be distributed all over the world, and added to that the structures of centralized planning and leadership of the "vanguard of the working class," the Communist party.

No doubt there are incompatibilities here. But it can also be pointed out that there are certain compatibilities. To the economists reality is very clear-cut. But *real* reality is not quite so bad as it sounds. Before I come to that, however, let me look at the other type of incompatibility.

And this is the interest part, which is much more concrete, much more material, if you will. It goes, roughly speaking, as follows: The Soviet Union has a geopolitical interest in having a tight, solid security belt around itself. In retrospect we can say that Soviet history, or Russian history rather, or both, is an exercise in constructing security belts, one outside the other. The Russian Soviet Federated Socialist Republic, today, can be seen as a security belt around what was once the Grand Duchy of Moscow. The Union of Soviet Socialist Republics, founded in 1922, can be seen as a security belt protecting the Russian Republic. The system of socialist countries can be seen as the third security belt, protecting the USSR. A glance at Soviet history will convince any unbiased reader that the idea of having a security belt was rooted in experience and not just in paranoia, as journalists in the West like to say.

Thus, a key U.S. ally, the Federal Republic of Germany, is the successor state to a state, the Third Reich, that had the idea not only of exterminating all European Jews but also the idea of exterminating, or at least enslaving, one hundred million Russians to pave the way for "Aryan" colonization. The Russians lost 20% of that number, and said NEVERMORE. Out of that came a geopolitical interest, custom-tailored to the expectation of a land war, with something quaint about it after the airplane was invented. But it is very deeply ingrained, as I have mentioned, in the Soviet military mind.

What corresponds to this on the Western and U.S. side is the socioeconomic interest in having the whole world as a place where property can be owned and property can be used productively to produce more property. That doctrine is known as free trade and free enterprise, originally based on property in the United States, then expanded to be valid for the whole world. For the United States it has some of the same apodictic, obvious quality as the geopolitical security doctrine has for the Soviet Union. For others it may taste unpleasantly, not of paranoia but of extreme greed.

If both of these doctrines are truly world encompassing, life becomes difficult for all of us. But neither of the superpowers has a reach so global that it can back up its demand that its doctrine be world encompassing. However, there was one particular part of the world where the incompatibility became crystal clear: Eastern Europe. The Soviet Union did not necessarily need a socialist Eastern Europe. It needed an Eastern Europe that would not once again turn fascist, against them. It should be remembered that Eastern European countries were Hitler's allies (with the major exception of Poland). And the United States did not necessarily need a democratic, capitalist Eastern Europe; it needed an Eastern Europe that was penetrable from an economic and social point of view. The geopolitical interests of the Soviet Union, as became clear after 1945, were definitely incompatible with the socioeconomic interests of the West in general, and the United States in particular. Moreover, there was the fear, probably totally unrealistic, that this unfortunate situation would, even soon, spread to the rest of Europe through Russian military expansionism, for instance in order to build a fourth security belt. I doubt that many seriously believe that today; and I have never found any evidence for such military plans.[5] For efforts to convert, and to some extent subvert, yes; but not military invasion.

Thus having formulated what, in my view, the conflicts are about, let us discuss conflict resolution; and then proceed to *B* and *A*. At the same time we must remember, when looking at the inter-East-West aspect, not to ignore the two intra-aspects. If we forget them we will come nowhere. Let us try, then, to solve the two inter-aspects of the conflict itself.

The easiest one is the struggle for power in Eastern Europe. If the Soviet Union's interest is geopolitical security, then that is better guaranteed by the Finnish solution than by the Polish, East German, Czech, Hungarian, Rumanian, and/or Bulgarian solutions. I myself have often heard in Moscow, and for a long time, that the best solution to the problem faced by the Soviet Union, having twelve countries bordering it from North Korea to Norway, is offered by Finland. The reason is very simple: Finland does not have a regime that has to be maintained by the bayonets of the Red Army, nor independent national communism. At the same time Finland has managed to make credible not only the obvious that no attack will emanate from Finland eastward, but also that Finland will stand up and defend itself against any transgressor who wants to make such an attack. This is more or less the way both parties read the Finnish-Soviet agreement of 1948—a treaty of security and friendship.

What I am saying now is that the Finnish-Soviet arrangement is probably the best model available for the solution to the dilemma of

Eastern Europe. Finlandization of Eastern Europe, in short. That the idea of "Finlandization" has not been understood in the United States is partly due to the low level of political education in the country, a problem that has to be taken seriously. The important point is that the Finnish social formation is at the same time open to the kind of reasonably formulated gains that capitalism, tempered by social democratic concerns, can produce. There is a dense social security net, and as much democracy as in any other Nordic country. In other words, the Finnish solution offers something in both directions. For that reason it was very logical that Finland hosted the fundamental Conference on Security and Cooperation in Europe (CSCE). And it was in Helsinki that the Final Act of Helsinki was signed, in 1975, exchanging geopolitical status quo for some commitment to human rights in the Soviet Union and economic cooperation (the three "baskets").

Finland stands at the crossroads, but in an equilibrium position due to real statesmanship. In no way does this mean neutralism in the sense that word is used in the United States. Neutralism does not mean that you are bland, "in-betweenish," when it comes to basic issues of liberal doctrine and values, for instance as enshrined in human rights. The Finns, like other Nordic peoples, stand very firmly on the first and second generation of human rights, the first generation of civil and political human rights of December 10, 1948, and the second generation of December 16, 1966 (less known in the United States and not yet ratified by the United States, like five other basic human rights covenants), of social, economic, and cultural human rights. Being in favor of both, the Finns can join the general Nordic approach of "plague on both your houses," since the United States is as weak on the second as the Soviet Union is on the first. That problem is well known in the Soviet Union but not in the United States. The Soviet weakness is increasingly discussed in the Soviet Union under the conditions of *glasnost'*. As I shall come to later, if and when *glasnost'* comes to the United States this will become public knowledge also there. The country infracts a major component of the International Bill of Rights daily.[6]

In short, there is a model, Finland, for the solution to the geopolitical and socioeconomic interest incompatibility. We then turn to the first aspect of the conflict, which was an incompatibility of basic values. Today it looks as if the superpowers have given up the ultimate strategy of making the whole world compatible or identical with their own ideological visions, or blueprints ("red print" in the case of the Soviet Union). They have seen that there are limits to expansion; there are hard cores of resistance. Those hard cores of resistance can be defined away as areas of irrelevance—as the United States has a tendency to do for Africa—or they can be defined as areas to "mature" later—as the Soviet Union has a tendency to do for the United States. But the point is that the push for the global reach is no longer there. Too much stands firmly in the way for that push to be realistic. Given that condition, we are again, to some extent, back to more regional battlefields: Europe, East and West, North and South. And in addition, some countries in East Asia—the second front of the Cold War, the Pacific theater.[7] That is also an East-West conflict, only that in the Pacific the eastern part is in the West and the western part is in the East.

What kind of compatibility do we find in spite of all this ideological noise? A very interesting one. If capitalism is defined in terms of giving priority to the market as the allocation mechanism for production factors and production decision, for distribution and consumption, and socialism is defined in terms of giving priority to central planning as the allocation mechanism; then the two are no longer so incompatible with each other as they might seem. It is only in the minds of some people in the United States and the Soviet Union that they are still incompatible.

We have today three very important alternatives to the "dark blue" market solution and the "dark red" central planning solution. We have the "rosa" solution of social democracy, in northern Europe and Canada, of a relatively weak compromise between market and plan. And here the name of the party in government is not so important. These are all essentially social democratic regimes with some small variations, and not very interesting variations at that, compared with the "blue" and the "red," the United States and the Soviet Union. Then we have the "golden" solution, a strong transcendence with 100% market and 100% plan as practiced by Japan, and increasingly successfully by a number of East Asian countries, the most important being, of course, the People's Republic of China. Big Government and Big Business run the game together. And we have an undercurrent of an informal economy, also in the United States, a "green" economy based on neither market nor plan in the nationwide sense. The "green" economy is based on barter, on a very limited nonexpanding economic cycle, and on producing things not for exchange but for own consumption. Above all the focus is on local economics; small supposedly being beautiful.

While the ideologues in the Soviet Union and particularly in the United States are fighting over the merits of the red and the blue, the world is experimenting with the rosa, the golden, and the green. This means that the superpowers are increasingly left by the wayside. The future belongs to the economy that is able successfully to integrate the three other solutions and produce good mixes of the mixes of market and plan.

In other words, the key to success may not even be the golden, rosa, or green; but combinations of the golden and the rosa and the green. That kind of debate is going on today in a number of countries in Eastern and Western Europe, in Europe North and South, and in a number of Third World countries. The debate is sneaking into the Soviet Union under *glasnost'* conditions and is still, practically speaking, unknown in the United States. Beginning on January 1 of 1988, even Soviet reality was changing, under *perestroika* conditions, dismantling the hegemony of the red model over the economy.

I would like to submit that much of the U.S. difficulty economically has to do with the inability to be more eclectic and up to date ideologically. The setback during the eight-year Reagan administration has been disastrous in this regard. What it comes down to is a focus on the middle range of economic systems that offers excellent compromises, to some extent even capable of transcending the incompatibilities that looked so unshakeable thirty years ago.

So, from both a geopolitical and socioeconomic interest point of view, and also from an ideological point of view the world has more to offer than the two classical superpower positions. In a sense, the conflict is dissolved or dissolving rather than being solved, though the last to realize it are Washington and Moscow. And today that sentence has to be modified further: the last to insist that there is still a very real conflict going on is the United States alone. But then this country can rightly point to still another terribly important part of the ideological conflict. What happens to democracy/dictatorship?

When it comes to experiments with new *economic* formations, the pilot country in Eastern Europe was, of course, Hungary. The decentralization of the 1960s to smaller units; the possibility of direct links between production companies so that they do not have to go via their respective ministries; shadow accounting in order to find out where the companies stand had they been working in a market econ-

omy and using the result of shadow accounting as a key to rewarding/
punishing the firm; the somewhat sporadic possibility of direct contact with firms abroad; higher priority to consumers—all of that has
been practised in the Hungarian economy for at least twenty years.
The reason why this has been going on for such a long time was pres-
sure from below: the Hungarian revolution of 1956, and the need for
a new party legitimacy within the geopolitical constraints. The process was stopped in Czechoslovakia in 1968 as we know, and is now
being resumed under *glasnost'* cultural conditions and the *perestroika* structural transformation. It is Eastern Europe that is moving
ahead, into eclecticism. And it is rather simplistic to try to understand what happens as merely a return to the profit motive and to private enterprise. There are elements of that, but there is also a search
for a third possibility. On the fringes of the system a lot of black mar-
keting/private profiteering is going on; but that is not where the
social formations as such are moving.

But what, then, about the basic political value dimension: democ-
racy/dictatorship? Again we have to turn to Hungary. What Hungary
did some years ago was to have the first open elections in a socialist
country. The choice was not between political parties; instead, for all
open positions there were two or three candidates. It was defined as a
step toward democracy with person-election rather than party-elec-
tion, a situation by no means unknown in a presidential democracy.
If this can be done at the top of the system it should be possible to do
so lower down too. It is not obvious that the last chapter in the book
of democracy and democratic theory has been written; a long list of
pros and cons about parties vs. persons can be given.

But the interesting point in Hungary was that when three people
were up for election, people who had been nominated at public
meetings with the heavy hand of the party in the background, there
was, nevertheless, a choice. And when the results were all in who
were elected? Was it the old, the middle-aged or the young? Was it
the party member or the nonparty member? Was it the woman or the
man? The answer is that people from all these categories were elected
—for example, on the basis of knowing the game of influence. But
there was one category which was clearly over-elected: medical doctors. It was a highly unanticipated consequence, both by liberal and
by marxist theory, that introduction of democracy in Eastern Europe
could mean that people no longer can find physicians because they
are doing politics! The explanation given by Hungarian sociologists

was that physicians were the only people in whom the electorate still had some modicum of trust. Evidently Hungarian doctors have been successful in impressing upon the population the idea that they are the people to be relied upon. I am not so sure that I, or anybody else for that matter, would like to see the American Medical Association as the alternative to present political conditions in the United States.

The serious point is that the Soviet Union is going to follow up, and already has imitated, what Hungary started. At the same time Bulgaria has declared, very clearly, that the preeminent position of the Communist party is coming to an end. Corresponding rules are being contemplated in the other countries—with the exception of Rumania, the most depressed and repressed country in all of Europe. Let me only add, parenthetically, that this is probably less because of socialism than because of the successful survival in Rumania of aspects of the Ottoman Empire, with Ceausescu himself in a sense being the last "sultan." The overthrow is now somewhat overdue.

In short, what in general looked so intractable some time ago seems now to be dissolving. There is a slow democratization process, and we are entering very important, even critical phases of the conflict resolution process. With the *C* corner of the *ABC* triangle for all practical purposes dissolving we are left with the question of what to do about *A* and *B*.

The conflict dissolves, yet the alliances and high armament levels survive. This is not rational. We have to move forward with alternative alliance systems, and alternative defense systems. The old "peace" slogans from the Cold War, *Disarmament Now!* and *Out of NATO!* will also have to be left by the wayside; they are not good enough. We need deeper thinking. The question is, What would be an alternative alliance system/alternative defense system? Let us look at the options as they are being discussed in Western Europe right now. And it is not necessarily only a European perception that there is no or little initiative in these matters coming from Washington. There seem to be four models of the future of the Western alliance in the political discussion in Western Europe, whereas in the United States most of this debate seems to be unknown.

First, there is of course the *status quo* option: the alliance, run in a hegemonial manner by the United States, continues roughly speaking as before. U.S. troops remain stationed in Western Europe; so do the bases.

Second, there is the European option of developing a strong, later on even autonomous, European alliance. The assumption would be not only withdrawal of U.S. troops, but also a gradual withdrawal of the U.S. nuclear umbrella, the INF agreement being a first step. Whether this is for military, political, or economic reasons, or any combination of them, matters less than the alternative: the gradual evolution[8] of the European Community (with the Western European Union) into a European superstate with the rights and duties of that construction, according to the current state-building pattern, of maintaining military forces commensurable with the political and economic power of the coming European community. France would play a leading role in this construction and in doing so would realize its old dream of interpreting *l'Europe des patries* as *l'Europe de Paris*. With France being the only continental power in Western Europe with independent nuclear arms, Paris will almost automatically become the center of a nuclear configuration, probably building on French-German cooperation and the special relationship France enjoys with her Latin neighbors to the south (Italy, Spain, Portugal). The particular status of France and Spain within the alliance as political but not fully fledged military members can then be used as a stepping-stone toward the development of a European superpower, independent of the United States. The nineteenth century recreated, before the year 2000!

Third, there is the distinct option, at present to some extent carried by Social Democratic[9] and Labor Parties,[10] of softening NATO and changing the military doctrine in the direction of defensive, nonprovocative defense. A number of proposals could be mentioned in this connection. Thus, there is the idea of a no-first use (nuclear) doctrine being accepted by the West, taking up the Soviet proposal of 1982. There is the idea of withdrawal of all foreign nuclear arms, a proposal which would in a certain sense play into the hands of France. This can then be supplemented with the Palme Commission proposal of withdrawing all weapons of mass destruction starting with a 300-kilometer border zone, particularly in Germany.

But there is also the much more fundamental idea of changing military doctrine to conventional arms alone, and pursuing this change further in the direction of nonprovocative conventional defense alone, possibly combined with paramilitary and nonmilitary defense.[11] All of this would then be for NATO as a whole, not only for the individual member countries. NATO would continue as a coordinating organization, among other reasons for conducting negotiations with the other side. But matters of defense would increasingly revert to the member states, under the doctrine of military self-reliance which is in itself a part of the doctrine of defensive defense.

Fourth, there is the radical pacifist option of developing the third option even further in the direction of abolishing NATO completely, together with the Warsaw Treaty Organization, thereby scrapping forever the "Yalta system" of division of Europe, and relying for defense matters on nonmilitary defense alone.

Politically, the first option is conservative, the second option is right-wing Social Democrat, the third option left-wing Social Democrat, and the fourth option green. This is not the place to speculate on the political future of these four options except to say that the first and the fourth are rather unlikely. Nothing will remain as it was after the Gorbachev revolution; however, Western Europeans are not yet ready for a really radical change.

The point that can be made is that unless there is a move in the direction of the third option a solution of the total conflict configuration is not around the corner. A Western European superpower would differ from an Atlantic superpower under hegemonial U.S. control mainly in one very negative regard: the center of gravity would be much closer to the Soviet Union. It seems to be in the nature of a superstate, and even more so a superpower, construction that it needs enemies in order to cohere. Military strength on the European continent is not very meaningful unless the enemy is at hand, meaning in Europe. And there is no other readily available candidate than the Soviet Union, meaning that the enemy construction and the long-lasting production of enemy images directed at the Soviet Union would have to continue in order to legitimize continued military build-up. At present, with Gorbachev, that model is in crisis. There might be strong forces favoring its reproduction.

Consequently, it is very much to be hoped that the second option will be rejected by the European peoples in their parliaments, even if the elites try to go ahead. But I am not optimistic in this regard since there are other values at stake that have nothing to do with the East-West conflict as such: the effort to construct the European superstate, with the European Community and the Western European Union as building blocs. And a superstate is a configuration with military build-up in one of the corners, regardless of whether it is needed for external purposes.

However, let us be optimistic and assume that this option aborts and that the third option in some form or another starts taking shape. This could be combined with the type of steps mentioned above in connection with conflict resolution. From the point of view of resolving the incompatibility of interests in Eastern Europe, the major points made were: "Finlandization" of Eastern Europe, meaning armed neutrality in the form of a nonprovocative defense standing up against efforts to change the status quo from either side; economic cooperation with both sides; political nonalignment; and a social security net sufficiently dense to prevent misery from reappearing in Eastern Europe. And correspondingly for the incompatibility of values: the road to resolution goes via the search and development of socioeconomic constructions that combine market and plan, as sketched above.

In all of this there is even an obvious solution for the two Germanys. The solution does not consist in a unified German *state,* a construction that was attempted twice, by Bismarck and by Hitler, and in some way or another a sufficient cause for the First and the Second World Wars to be a social experiment the rest of Europe would not like to see replicated; but in the reunification of the German *nation,* under a slogan such as "It should be as easy to travel from Bavaria in West Germany to Thüringen in East Germany as from Bavaria to Tirol in Austria." That is, the free flow of persons, goods/services, and ideas. And the moves these recent years are certainly in that direction, at an accelerating pace.

But to that should be added an important political point that could bring peace to Europe almost with one stroke: the wall surrounding West Berlin has to go. So has the fence erected by the East Germans all along the border. But West Germany also has to give up something: the claim to be the only German successor state to the preceding German constructions (that anybody can want to be the successor state to the Nazi regime remains enigmatic). Both anomalies come out of the Cold War. Why not trade one for the other, abolishing at once the wall, the fence, and the doctrine of the successor state, letting the two Germanys be precisely that, two Germanys, with a completely normal relationship, separate but equal, fully respecting each other?

Needless to say, all of this would have to take place both on the Western and on the Eastern side. And that seems today less problematic. There are already conferences in the East discussing the possibility of less coupling, both politically and militarily, of the Eastern

countries to the Soviet Union. And there is in the Soviet Union interest in basic change of military doctrine.¹² In other words, it may very
well be that the West will have to catch up with the East rather than
vice versa.

But what could happen between the alliances in addition to count-
less negotiations about these matters? Two points should be mentioned. Both have a ring of the obvious within the logic of this
scheme.

First, there is people's diplomacy in addition to governmental and
in general elite diplomacy. The United States has made important
strides forward in this regard. The number of United States groups
propagating better relations with the Soviet Union, organizing travel
groups, conferences, TV bridges, and what not, is astounding. This is
all to the good. It is educational; direct human links are being
created, a web of peace is spun sufficiently strong to withstand even
high amounts of tension that inevitably will come on the bumpy road
ahead of us.

Second, there should be some basic pattern of positive cooperation, country to country, between the two superpowers since they are
the nuclei of the conflict. What can the United States give to the
Soviet Union and what can the Soviet Union give to the United
States? Of course, they might exchange electricity over the Bering
Strait, making a dense electric grid as a model of a peace grid. The
proposal has the great advantage that the same kind of thing would
go from one to the other in both directions: it is not the old pattern
of "cooperation," with West extracting raw materials from East thus
creating dependencies in the East on Western sophisticated goods in
return. Incidentally, this is a pattern firmly rejected by Gorbachev.

But we should try to do something better than that. Moreover,
there should be elements of "people-to-people" cooperation, and
many of them, not only goods/services exchanged for goods/services.
Could it be that something relatively labor-intensive exists on which
one country is doing fine and has a surplus and the other country is
not doing so well and could make use of some additional labor force?
I suggest that there are two such gaps that could be bridged.

Soviet agriculture is highly deficient, and the United States has an
agricultural system so efficient that it has painted itself into the corner of substantial crisis in the farm belt because of overproduction.
How about offering the Soviet Union 10,000 U.S. farmers who could
act as consultants, as middle-level humanpower in the crumbling *sov-*

khozi and *kolhozi* all around the Soviet Union, giving practical advice, trying to reintroduce agricultural skills in an agricultural population de-skilled both by the Stalinist crimes against the rural population and by excessive planning from above? A genuine act of friendship, people to people!

What should the Soviet Union do in return? Where is the American deficit that could be compared with this? The immediate answer would be in class terms: there is a misery at the bottom of U.S. society not found at the bottom of Soviet society. But it would hardly be politically possible to call in Soviet advisors to work on restructuring U.S. class society in such a fundamental way. However, Soviet advisors might have some interesting ideas about how to spin a dense network of people-centers, cultural clubs, and things of that kind in order to give meaningful alternatives to the delinquent subcultures with drug and narcotic overtones.

But there is still another possibility. If the Soviet Union has a food deficit, the United States has a mental food deficit of a very particular kind: knowledge of the world. Why not send 10,000 Soviet students, teachers, and students in teachers' colleges to the United States to teach classes around the country? The level of fluency in the English language is remarkably high in the Soviet Union these recent years. These Soviet teachers would, of course, be expected to teach elements of Russian and Soviet history and general knowledge of the Soviet Union. They could also teach some useful Russian, the goal not being to train a number of Americans to perfection in that language, but to give them a taste of a beautiful idiom different from their own. But most important, they could simply teach world history and world geography as they see it. Much can be said about the distorted way in which this teaching is done in U.S. schools today. Why not give U.S. pupils a different version and the chance to make out for themselves what would be a more valid view of world history and geography, and not only adding the U.S. version to the Soviet version, but dividing by two.

Finally, then, we come to *A* for attitude. According to the scheme, it divides into two parts: the inter-aspect and the intra-aspect.

The inter-aspect obviously has to do with the *Feindbilder,* the images of the enemy. Carl Sagan has circulated around the United States an article, which was also published in the Soviet Union, exploring the relationship between the two nations. It showed images replete with distortions, filled with "nightmare images of the other, used in each nation to maintain continuing enmity."[13] But Sagan also rightly points out that these images are not totally without foundation. Atrocities have been and are being committed by both sides. To try to conceal this fact will always backfire; sooner or later they are brought up again. Much more useful is to discuss them rationally, to permit oneself to be exposed to criticism from the outside, and try to learn from it.

However, missing in this type of analysis of the image of Other is the image of Self; in other words, the intra-aspect. As mentioned at the beginning of this chapter, the problem is neither the image of the Other nor the image of Self alone, but the combination of the two. It is when the gradient between a highly inflated Self-image and a highly dehumanized Other-image becomes too steep that we are in real trouble. In other words, it is not enough for the United States and the Soviet Union to have joint conferences to adjust textbooks about each other.[14] The two superpowers are also called upon, and not only by the rest of the world but also by responsible opposition within the two countries, to adjust images they have of themselves (including textbooks about themselves).

More particularly, I think the United States gets into much of its difficulties precisely because of its Self-definition as God's own country, as chosen by God to bring Americanization to a waiting human-kind.[15] That some individuals cannot wait but become so eager that they emigrate to the United States is taken as evidence that the image is correct. With such ideas of oneself it becomes not only a right but a duty to bring Americanization and *pax americana,* particularly to the Western Hemisphere.

But the Soviet Union has a corresponding Self-image. Being at present headed by an atheist regime, the nation is not chosen by God but by History as the first country entering the territory of socialism, and with not only the right but also the duty to show the world what blessings lie ahead. I have no objection to the second socialist revolution under Gorbachev as an effort to build a better socialism. What would be objectionable would be if Gorbachev sees this as a way of continuing Soviet hegemony by his country being not only the guiding beacon, but also the country that has the right and indeed the duty to ease the transition of others into the realm of socialism.

In short, let each country develop according to its own inclinations. Let each superpower become as beautiful as it can, so that people can come to its shores, and even farther, gazing into the land, admiring and learning what they want to learn. But let neither superpower develop the idea that it is entitled not only to a missionary zeal but to use its military and economic power to conduct crusades and anticrusades to spread its pattern all over the world. For that is, I am afraid, the nucleus of the whole East-West conflict.

CHAPTER 2

The "North-South" Conflict

In this chapter I shall develop six themes that have to do with solving the North-South conflict. Let me start by giving you my list of six topics, although they will not necessarily be dealt with in this order.

1. A general diagnosis of the nature of the North-South conflict.
2. A return to the triangular definition of conflict in terms of attitude *(A)*, behavior *(B)*, and conflict *(C)* from chapter 1 on the East-West conflict, also using the intra/inter distinction.
3. A five-stage approach to the solution: consciousness, mobilization, confrontation, struggle, and self-reliance, with some delinking and then relinking, on an equitable basis.
4. A "spelling out" of the fifth stage which has to do with a theory of self-reliance, based on the idea of equity.
5. An effort to explore the noneconomic aspects of the North-South conflict, because "North-South" generally means economic problems. Here again are the quotation marks, as at the beginning of chapter 1. The conflict is mainly between the world Northwest and the Third World, not with the industrialized "North" in general.
6. An exploration of how this relates to the United States and Japan. The United States, since the beginning of the 1980s, has maneuvered itself into the position of a Third World country relative to Japan and is no longer a real First World country. This is a new role for the United States, as "hewers of wood and drawers of water," of scrap iron and waste paper and some foodstuffs, in return for very sophisticated manufactures. Hence I shall use Japan-United States as an example, not—as is usual—

United States-South America, European Community-Africa, Japan-Southeast Asia, etc.

Let me start with the diagnosis. The North-South conflict is *vertical*. The East-West conflict is *horizontal*. These are a couple of very heady terms, so let me spell them out. In the East-West conflict we have, roughly speaking, parties of the same kind confronting each other across a border. They know what they want and they have their strategies. The conflict border is geographical more than social. Of course, there are two or three classes of nations, divided as superpowers, big powers, and clients; and two classes of people, divided as elites and ordinary people. But there is a certain homogeneity on both sides. They are standing looking at each other, sometimes in a very hostile way, eyeball to eyeball, sometimes gun to gun.

The Soviet foreign minister and the U.S. foreign minister both agreed about one thing: they should take a critical look at the hostile images they have of each other and try to do something about them. The assumption was that there are two parties, just two. As I have said earlier, this critical review is important. But even more important is a critical look at the images they have of themselves. If you have a self-inflated image of yourself and a denigrating one of the other, and the other side has exactly the same view from the very opposite vantage point, then we are in for trouble. This belongs to the analysis of East-West relations and is rather important.

But in the verticality of the much more complex North-South conflict we always have to distinguish between at least four parties. There is the center country and the periphery country, and a center in the center country, and a periphery in the center country. Roughly speaking, the people in the center are in command, the elites; and the ordinary people are in the periphery. There are also elites in the periphery country and nonelites, ordinary people, in the periphery country. And the four groups are not unrelated. If there is an alliance between the two elites then that is a rather fundamental aspect of the total configuration, a kingpin of what is known as imperialism. And this is the basic configuration underlying the North-South conflict.[1]

To build on this point I now jump straight to number 6 on the list to see better how the Japanese are building that alliance between Japanese and U.S. elites. The thesis is that Japan-U.S. relations are, today, as good an example of economic imperialism, or "North-South" conflict, as any.

In order to penetrate the United States, linking elites together, there are two basic methods Japan can use—and neither of them works in Europe. To make that very clear let us ask what is needed to control a country in Europe. There is only one way: through political parties. But the political parties are reserved for the countries' own nationals. In the United States political parties play a minor role. But there are two other openings, one of them narrow, one wide. The first is lobbying in Washington, in the legislative and/or the executive branches. (In European countries the major lobby is the political party on top of every single individual point of view.) The other method of penetrating the United States is investing in the soft underbelly of the individual states, and these gateways are wide open. The gateway called Hawaii is one very clear example. But more important are the states from Ohio southward.

What the Japanese have to do is to forge solid links with local elites, ranging from politicians to real estate agents to golf club owners to CEOs in joint ventures. It can be done, for instance, by appealing to them as sellers with sellers' interests.[2] It is incredible how much difference ten, fifteen, twenty years of working at this kind of bridgehead-building can make to relative power. The formula is standard in the North-South conflict in general. All one has to get used to is seeing the United States in the role of the periphery, not in the center role it plays south of the Rio Grande.

What makes this total relation vertical is that the center country gets much more out of it than does the periphery country. The technical/nontechnical word for "getting much more out of it" is exploitation.[3] The basic key to exploitation is vertical division of labor, meaning that when the products exchanged in the bargain are ranked in terms of degree of processing—the amount of capital, research, and management that go into the products, as opposed to raw materials and unskilled labor—and in terms of the challenges built into the job of creating the product, then the center gets much more positive spin-off effects, value added, and much more challenge than does the periphery.

The division of labor will show up in the composition of trade, with the (Japanese) center exporting sophisticated products, like excellent cars and motorbikes, machine tools, electronics, and computers; and the (United States) periphery exporting such products as soy beans and agricultural products, waste paper, and scrap iron. I would like to add that no self-respecting Asian/African/South American or generally Third World country has come down to the level of scrap iron and waste paper. They usually stay at the level of iron ore, even bauxite, cotton bales, crude sugar.

Of course the United States is also exporting sophisticated arms, passenger aircraft, computers, and services. That means that Japan has four jobs remaining to complete the vertical configuration. By making the configuration complete they push the United States further down the vertical division-of-labor ladder defined by degree of processing. Let me therefore make four predictions that are rather obvious. *Point one:* Japan will increasingly produce its own arms, trying to do it in such a way as not to arouse world suspicion. *Point two:* Japan will produce her own passenger aircraft, specifically pollution-free and noise-free, short range, STOL passenger aircraft for ninety to one hundred passengers. From this we can predict a coming U.S. unemployment pattern around Boeing in the Seattle area and around McDonnell-Douglas in St. Louis, Missouri. *Point three:* Japan will eventually take over IBM, as a daughter company. This is a rather precise prediction that I have made since 1983, with 1993 as the deadline. In a bet I made with IBM managers, I insisted the bet should be in yen, not in dollars, and I do not repent that.[4] Finally, *point four:* Japan will continue making inroads in the vast U.S. service market, from hotels to securities and beyond.

I will now develop this argument further by looking at the joint construction of an exploitative pattern, based on a coalition between the two centers. To build that coalition Japan has to do a bit more work. It has to convince at least twenty-six states in the union that it is in their best interest to continue to be exploited. The moment Japan has these twenty-six states it will have a majority in the U.S. Senate. If I were Japan bent on this exercise I would do the following: I would look at an economic atlas of the United States of America and conclude that in a bicoastal economy one should stay away from the coasts, except for tourism and real estate. It is in the middle of the country that land is cheap, labor is cheap, and the states are in economic difficulties. I would invest from the Great Lakes down to the Gulf of Mexico. Maybe I would start in Tennessee and Kentucky, spread to Ohio and Missouri, and go southward. I would be very much interested in extremely cheap acreage, and in labor costs below the national average. I would do my little homework, paying my U.S. consultants handsomely. I would count as success number 1 that the governor of Ohio in September 1987 instructed the Ohio delegation not to vote for sanctions against Japan. I would score "one." Relatively quickly afterward I could score "six"; there were more states in the same category. And I would have some foundations pour out money for Japan studies at United States and European universities to exercise some control over the production of Japan images.

All these are among the elementary building blocs in forging a North-South conflict. Great Britain (or the former Great Britain; I mean United Kingdom, formerly united, still a queendom), France, and other countries of that kind have been doing this for some time. The United States has also been doing exactly this for some time, particularly south of the Rio Grande. And so, down the road, as this pattern is evolving, we may see the kidnapping of Japanese businessmen, demonstrations, boycott of Japanese goods, and confrontations that might become much more bitter than anything we have seen so far. As a peace researcher I am not primarily talking about bad Japan-U.S. relations because of concerns with the U.S. economy. I am concerned with the general state of world health, meaning peace. I see nasty conflicts building up, with nasty manifestations.

The problem is that a vertical conflict may look so peaceful that the luxury of misunderstanding it systematically seems affordable. The debate in recent years has given in to much talk about "trade deficit," which is the discourse that fills U.S. media. But there is nothing wrong in having a trade deficit in bilateral relations. Nothing, either in trade theory or in peace theory, rules out owing somebody money, as long as you have a trade surplus with somebody else and can use that surplus to cancel the debt. This is called "multilateral clearing" and is an important contribution to making world trade rational. If we should clear the accounts in all bilateral arrangements singly, not combined, we would almost be back to the barter level of trade and exchange in general.

Having said that, we of course come to the conclusion that the problem for the United States is not a trade deficit of 60–70 billion dollars relative to Japan. The problem is a trade deficit, with practically speaking every country that matters. And one reason for that is very simple: the United States is increasingly in the position of a Third World country, having very little to export of sufficient quality to fetch a good price on the world market. There are exceptions, such as McDonald's Hamburgers and Kentucky Fried Chicken, contributing to a more equal distribution around the world of fundamentally unhealthy food. This way the danger to the human body can be distributed in a more equitable manner, and not show up mainly in the country from where it comes. But it is not a way of solving the United States economic problems, nor the problems of world peace.

The United States is in a rather precarious situation economically, not unlike the situation of Third World countries. The problem is how to get out of this situation, which is not going to be easy. In general we find U.S. business elites, willing real estate agents and sellers, and many others already in collusion with the Japanese elites. Add to this analysis that Japan has been doing this for only about a century, whereas the Western powers have spent about 500 years practising economic imperialism. Of course, the Japanese are often more skillful than the West, so we would not expect them to need 500 years to build a worldwide system of economic penetration. They are good students. They are also in search of more justice in the world. When the Japanese find themselves accused of causing economic conflicts around the world they have an argument: "Is this wrong? But the West has been doing this all the time! Why is it wrong only when we do it?" It is very interesting in international conferences to watch American delegates trying to handle that line of thought. They generally do not manage, being neither intellectually nor morally up to the task, but start threatening Japan with sanctions.

From this diagnosis using Japan-U.S. as an example of the North-South conflict, let us proceed to the five stages of conflict resolution. The five stages have as their point of departure consciousness-formation (attitude!), mobilization (behavior!), and confrontation. Consciousness-formation occurs as people get a sense of somebody being short-shrifted, in other words, of exploitation. And this hits both inter and intra, between Japan and the United States, and within the United States. As an example of what it means within the United States, look at Hawaii press reports on March 2, 1988.[5] Farmers and farm devoted people, evaluating the relative need for a golf course and farmland, are demonstrating in favor of the latter. The argument that there is Japanese capital behind a substantial number of golf courses is brought in. The argument that it is difficult to eat golf balls (NO CAN EAT GOLF BALLS) is very prominent. The health consequences might prove disastrous.

I have seen similar demonstrations many times in South American and in Asian countries, with exactly the same arguments. I have also seen that the British, French, or American owners, etc., were not on the scene; nor were the Japanese in Hawaii. They were safe, probably back home. I have seen the police taming the demonstrators, but not turning their power the opposite way. Police have some ability to stay the hand of a demonstrator with water cannons, police horses and dogs, gas. But imagine the effect of a water cannon in the investor's office, or in the office of the real estate agent, including its impact on documents. The forces of public order and the military tend to be on the side of the strong, not of the weak. This usually comes out clearly in the confrontation that follows a mobilization, even in a mild demonstration. And it adds to the consciousness about the conflict by crystallizing the issue.

A vertical conflict is a conflict between strong and weak over the continuation of an inequitable structure. Of course this has an impact on attitude and behavior. I mentioned demonstrations, a typical but rather weak form of vertical conflict behavior. Down the road there is considerably more dramatic behavior. Sooner or later a pattern emerges of repetitive and persistent acts of confrontation. Certificates of terrorism are then issued from above. Now some comments on this term must be made.

Terrorism from below is the weapon of the weak. The terrorist fights in a very particular way. He cannot afford to appear in open battle, inviting massive retaliation. What he has to do is to appear now and then, but not in-between; and here and there, but not in-between. In other words, the basic tactic of terrorists is discontinuity in time and noncontiguity in space—making themselves unpredictable. The major weapon is unpredictability and that is what makes terrorism terrible, not the horrors of violence. The numbers killed by terrorism in recent years is only a couple of hundreds a year, in other words nothing relative to U.S.-sponsored state terrorism in Nicaragua. The latter is carried out by the contras, financed by the United States, partly from public, partly from semipublic funds, and partly from private funds (like Pat Robertson's, through his Christian Broadcasting Network, CBN). In short, terrorism from below and state terrorism from above—combined with torturism and death squads and "low intensity conflict"—are to vertical, asymmetrical conflicts what regular warfare is to horizontal symmetrical conflict. But this is hardly the future of Japan-U.S. relations.

However, if we turn to attitude, to the *A* part of the triangle and to the two parts we are concerned with—emotional and cognitive—Japan-U.S. relations may serve as an example. Emotions start getting hot. The anti-American sentiment in Japan is already high,[6] and the anti-Japanese sentiment in the United States is coming. The cognitive aspect, "consciousness," the ability to understand the patterns operating in the conflict, is still lagging behind, particularly in the United States. The consciousness I have been arguing so far has a marxist tinge. Maybe 5% marxism is needed for an understanding of what is going on. But in the present intellectual/political atmosphere in the United States, 5% marxism would be exactly 5% too much. Low consciousness in the United States about what happens gives Japan a tremendous advantage. South America is not as poorly equipped in consciousness relative to the United States as the United States is relative to Japan. And the United States problem is painfully obvious: consciousness in the Japan-U.S. relationship is blocked by the awesome perspective of admitting at least some validity to the South American perspective in the United States.

Consciousness is indispensable to giving an answer to the basic problem, What to do about it. Only through consciousness can the natural-law quality of structural violence erupting into direct violence be superseded. But consciousness or ideology should not only tell us what is wrong, it should also indicate an alternative. My general proposals are two new economic theories/practices that I will refer to as *self-reliance I* and *self-reliance II*.[7] Self-reliance I simply means to produce goods and services oneself, regionally, nationally, locally, rather than getting them through trade or aid from more "advanced" regions, nations, districts. The point is to make use of whatever exists of raw materials, labor, capital, technology, management; not to make products for export but to provide for own needs. The challenge of producing to the maximum, precisely to develop while creating rather than just buying or getting, is fully accepted. This is often called "import-substitution" as if import were normal. How about referring to import as "self-reliance substitution"?

But what if there are no raw materials? The Japan-U.S. example also serves to show that there might be more to raw materials than the quest for economic profitability, making so many dig more deeply into mountains to find more. It may also be that it is in a nation's narrow interest *not* to dig too deeply, but to announce to the world that it has no raw materials available, so as to legitimize a high position in the vertical division of labor, setting itself up as manufacturer for others, using the raw materials of others. In that case the nation would not be able to get manufactured goods in exchange for raw materials. It would have to make them itself. It would be forced, or would force itself, to be challenged, relying on human creativity.

After self-reliance I comes self-reliance II. Self-reliance II is exchange, but on the basis of equity. But how does one do that? Here we have to go more deeply into the matter, and the essence of the matter, in my view, lies in all the things economists cannot or refuse to handle intellectually in their theories. But the economists, in one sense, are honest. They have a word for what they have left out: externalities, thereby indicating that what is external to the economist's theory is also external in the sense of being marginal in relevance. In doing so they imply that an economist's brain is relatively central in the universe; other people are handling peripheral matters.[8]

So let us now just do the opposite; let us push the economist's brain aside and look at the externalities. Externalities are the unaccounted, positive and negative, effects of economic activities. Sometimes, but usually not, they may be costed, monetized. To cost the negative externalities we have to ask the question, How much would it cost to repair the damage? To cost the positive externalities we have to ask the question, How much would I have to pay to get this advantage without engaging in that economic activity?

To make a simple list of externalities let us divide the world into four spaces: nature space, human space, social space, world space. The externalities in nature space are essentially negative and known as pollution and depletion, as two relatively shallow aspects of ecological degradation. The trick in classical capitalistic practice (not admitted in theory) is to push the negative externalities onto the trade partners. One way of doing that is to move the industries to the trade partner, like putting Japanese smokestacks in Ohio. The West has been doing that for ages; the new element is only that now Japan is doing it, in the West. And I already mentioned the role of the Ohio governor in that connection.

In human space a key positive externality is challenge: to process uncertainty into certainty; to process chaos into structure is what research, science, is about. It is also what manufacturing is about, taking a lump of raw material, giving it shape, like making a carburetor—in the old days the epitome of achievement. Today, of course, it would be an IC, an integrated circuit, a superconductor. The negative externality lies in what may happen to the human body, mind, and spirit in the process: cardiovascular diseases, malignant tumors, mental disorders, and the general sense of alienation, all of which seem to follow in the wake of so much industrial activity. The more negative externality we have, the more drugs of various kinds we need. This negative externality does not necessarily come from trade-related industry. It could also come from our domestic industrial activity; from economic activity in general, not necessarily from the import-export oriented sector.

In social space the negative externality would be a heavily class-divided nonparticipatory society and a very immobile social order as the almost inevitable result of being at the bottom of the vertical conflict formation I have described between center and periphery, between and within countries. I would imagine that down the road in Japan, and in the United States, there will be an upper class between the Great Lakes and the Gulf of Mexico sending its sons and daughters to Japan for study, eating considerably more than *sushi* three times a day, talking some Japanese, participating regularly in *ikebana* competitions—which is not the worst thing one can do—having all their children doing *aikido* and *karate,* and in general being well Japanized like so many English, French, United States-oriented imitators all over the world.

The ritual trip to Tokyo will be the high point of the annual cycle for these Japanized Americans. They will have special guest rooms with *tatami* floors. Their apartments in the United States are already prepared: it has been calculated that in apartments in Manhattan more than two-thirds of the value put inside comes from Japan, and from East Asia in general. That, of course, does not mean that there are not also U.S.-made things like mattresses, maybe a bed, a couple of chairs, and simple things of that kind. I am not saying that less mobility in society, low participation in decision making, and less opening of closed gates for the dispossessed and underprivileged is inevitable, only that it is down the road. It is not so easy to fight absentee owners in Tokyo. The center country may perhaps function as an engine pulling other national economies. But what does that amount to if the third-class cars for common people are not hitched onto the train, but are left behind on a side track?

The major negative externality in world space are the international conflicts that sooner or later come out of economic activity of the type discussed. It speaks badly for the intellectual tradition of economists that they have permitted themselves to go ahead with their theories

of comparative advantages without being forced to consider peace/
war implications. Of course, not all the blame should be laid at the
feet of economists. It should also accrue to those willing to demand
"economics as usual," like the economists giving each other Nobel
prizes for achievements guided by this self-imposed but rather extensive blindness. It should give some food for thought that economists
of the (neo)classical kind are so easily employable in military auto-
cratic regimes, with heavy nonparticipatory social formations, and
violent conflicts with other countries.

The corresponding positive externality would come out of the type
of economic relationship that is both symbiotic and equitable, with
built-in conflict resolution mechanisms, so that both parties gain
about equally. Peace is built into the process. There are three areas in
the world where such intercountry positive externalities seem to dom-
inate over the negative ones: the twelve European Community countries among themselves (but not relative to the rest of the world); the
six ASEAN countries (Association of Southeast Asian Nations); and,
as you would expect from a Nordic chauvinist, the five Nordic countries. A total of twenty-three countries with about 620 million inhabitants.

A good example of the opposite would be the U.S.-Canada relationship, in my view heading for open conflict. The residual *pax
americana* promoted by the Reagan administration today seems ulti-
mately to aim at a free trade area from Tierra del Fuego to Hudson
Bay. But a free trade area between an elephant and some mosquitoes
can be very tough for the mosquitoes in the first run; later on possibly
for the elephant. In order to push this pattern through, the United
States needs eager, cooperative elites in the other countries; in Canada, Toronto businessmen, and in Ottawa, parliamentarians in collusion with Toronto businessmen. Whether that will work in Canada
the way Washington wants is not obvious. It has worked economically, but not psycho-politically in South America. To the extent that
the pattern can be relied upon, the South American country, from
the Washington point of view, is ripe for democracy (if not, it is in for
"destabilization"). Democracy can be declared, elections can be
held. Obviously, Nicaragua stands in the way; possibly also Panamá.
And what is the United States' conclusion? Pay the contras, send the
marines; threaten with either.

Imagine now the total sum of positive and negative externalities
and you get a picture of the total exploitation. If we want to solve the

North-South conflicts, the economic relationship has to be built in such a way that the externalities come out (1) more positively and (2) more equitably. That gives us two basic points in the theory of self-reliance: (1) minimize the negative and enhance the positive externalities; (2) share the net (positive minus negative) externalities equally. The most exploitative pattern, as mentioned, is to push all the negative externalities onto somebody else, retaining the positive externalities for oneself. And that, I am afraid, is the major reason why economists leave out the externalities. They are not stupid; it is not that they do not know that externalities matter. But they have an implicit pact with the establishment not to mention the unmentionable; not to speak the unspeakable. Pushing these points you will find tenured economics professor Dr. X saying, "Of course it is like that. But you know I cannot say it; there will be no funding available." If he does not have tenure yet, economist Dr. Y will say, "I will not get my tenure." They are probably both right.

Self-reliance I and self-reliance II are exactly what is practiced in the three peace areas I mentioned. The reason is that the member countries have another pact: Either we hang together, we hang separately, or we hang each other in the often miserable European way. All three areas have built into them a common purpose: we will build economic relations in such a way that it is peace-productive among ourselves. My experience as a consultant is that making these externality points in those three areas is like pushing through open doors; they are conscious about it. The only thing a person like me can do is to give them the intellectual rationale for what they are doing anyhow. It is like Molière and the man who has been talking prose all the time. Some of them say, "I didn't know I was exercising all that wisdom. So, I am a peace practitioner?"

The point is, of course, that nobody in his or her right mind would practice comparative advantages theory on friends. With friends you are considerate; you help them along. Friendly relations are not relationships with solid built-in interests in retaining exploitation. I think it can be proven relatively simply that in the longer run we are all served by equitable, friendly, economic relationships, with the two interpretations I mentioned: minimizing the negative externalities and sharing the net sum of externalities equally. But to do that we have to reconstruct economic theory in general, and trade theory in particular. Both are issues too important to be left to economists of the traditional kind.

Let me now look at vertical conflict in the light of power: economic, political, military, and cultural. The clever craftsman empire-builder does not use openly police or military power. The clever one builds a structure which can sustain the exploitation by itself. The First World is reported to bring about 40 billion dollars in various ways into the Third World, getting back about 150 billion dollars, annually. There are very many mechanisms through which this happens, essentially built around the harmony of interests I mentioned between the two elites. But a couple of other factors are also needed. One useful factor is to reduce the consciousness and mobilization levels lower down in society. This is best accomplished by exercising cultural power (like "the meek shall inherit the earth") or, in the vulgar case, unadulterated censorship. When that no longer works so that the economic power does not function sufficiently well, there is often a spill-over to the political and military dimensions.

What is happening right now in Central America is that the United States is trying to get rid of one obstacle to the project of a free trade area from Tierra del Fuego to Hudson Bay: cooperatives run by the people of Nicaragua, working in the countryside and also operating clinics and schools. The U.S.-financed contras do not attack Sandinista military goals so much as precisely cooperatives, destroying the alternatives, the buildings and the simple machines, killing the farmers, the women, the children; spreading terror. The leader of the contras, Mr. Calero, who had the Coca Cola franchise in Nicaragua under Somoza and has been on the CIA payroll, was a clear embodiment of that structure.

I mentioned cultural power, and one aspect is social theory. Some element of essentially marxist analysis is indispensable in understanding exploitation, although I think marxism can be improved upon considerably with externality theory and self-reliance proposals. And there are some other phenomena marxism does not explain well at all. One such point is that imperialism tends to continue even when the imperialists lose economically. In other words, marxism also suffers from an overdose of the spirit of the business accountant. Are we in the black? Are we in the red? Are we short-shrifted? What are the opportunity costs? How can we continue being in the black? The point is that some countries, like the United States in Central America, fight to maintain the structure even when they are in the red, with costly military-political operations, because they are driven by another script than that attributed to them by the marxist type of rationality. They are Chosen People, anointed. There is a script saying they are preordained to rule a certain part of the world. To be anointed carries with it the obligation to purge the territory of evil influences, leaving the good forces to rule alone.

This double perspective, economic and cultural, has an added advantage which marxist rationality does not have. If all of this were done for money alone the whole U.S. population could never be mobilized. The trickling-down effect inside U.S. society is insufficient, particularly under the present regime. An immediate sharing of the spoils could mobilize the population along economic lines; but we know perfectly well that most of the money derived from that type of activity is not well distributed. If it were, there would not be 20 million hungry in the United States, 40 million below the poverty line, and 10,000 shelterless in New York alone. Given that fact, the bottom part of the population has to be mobilized by other means. And that is where we get the basic formula for Reaganism: Reaganism equals military/corporate greed plus right-wing populism. It is not a bad formula; it comes from Noam Chomsky.[9] I think the right-wing populism in the United States is essentially written in theological script, but I will not develop that point further.[10]

Let me now summarize, since point six, using U.S.-Japan relations as an example, has been spread over all the other five points. To solve the North-South conflict means working tenaciously, systematically, for a new world economic relationship, here called self-reliance I and self-reliance II. Self-reliance I implies being competitive in your own country by doing your utmost to use your own production factors, including developing them further. It may also imply selective delinking and some protectionism. Self-reliance II enters the scene when self-reliance I has met with its limits: engage in trade, but in an equitable way, meaning sharing externalities equally. If you have delinked, relink but on an equitable basis.

One way of being equitable is to trade within the primary, secondary, and tertiary sectors instead of between the sectors. One sure recipe for inequity is to trade manufactured goods against primary commodities. So trade must mean manufactured goods against manufactured goods and agricultural goods against agricultural goods. Services should be organized in terms of their spin-off effects and defects, and exchanged so that the net spin-offs, or externalities, come out about the same.

If the economists cannot tell us how this is done, change the economists, challenge them, or retrain them. One mechanism that I would suggest would be to hitch the salaries of economists to the level of unemployment (not counting junk labor producing junk goods/services as full employment), or to the deficit. I would also hitch it, I think, to the value of the dollar. That would make it possible to get out of one particular dilemma, namely, that in the midst of this conflict formation there is a profession that gets off scot-free regardless of the number of accumulated mistakes they have made, with schools of thought that seem to go particularly well with military dictatorships —such as the Chicago School in Pinochet Chile.

In addition to this effort to solve the conflict, raise the level of consciousness. To raise the level of consciousness in the United States access to the media for countertrend analysis is indispensable. I would imagine that to be an uphill task if what is needed is to create alternative views, made even worse by the mind-set dominating U.S. media people in this field.[11]

In addition, make it an international crime to participate in wars fought abroad to maintain inequitable economic structures. Make that crime punishable at least in the sense that the names of the participants are made known internationally. I am thinking of mercenaries, and I am thinking of exactly the same type of international law as is today being constructed around torturism—making torture an international crime. More constructively, organize joint economic activity in such a way that it becomes unobjectionable to all parties concerned and there is no need to "send the marines" to "protect our economic interests abroad."[12]

And finally, have a look at those cultural factors that seem to justify this kind of conflict behavior. The inflated Self-image; the deflated Other-image. If you look at the totality of that, including the latter-day version in terms of "more developed"/"less developed," and "we" have to develop "them," it becomes clear that the North-South conflict is much more difficult than the East-West conflict in the sense that intellectually it requires much more of all of us, including a thorough revision of mainstream economic theory. There is so much at stake, like the whole idea of "modernization."

In conclusion: North-South conflicts differ fundamentally from East-West conflicts. The latter may call for third parties who may say "plague on both your houses" or "you are both right" and help the parties toward a compromise. The North-South conflict is emotionally simpler. The down-trodden and the exploited call for solidarity on our part. The oppressors are also to be pitied as moral victims of the structure in which they are entrapped. But our function is to change that structure toward a more equitable one; and in the shorter run, that will mean some losses for the exploiters. In the longer run, it may bring gains for all. It is in the interest of all of us that we plan for the longer run.

CHAPTER 3

The "Middle East" Conflict

Let us start with the beginning, literally speaking, with Genesis
15:18:

> So that day Jehovah made this covenant with Abram: "I have given
> this land to your descendants from the Wadi-el-Arish to the river
> Euphrates. And I give to them these nations: Kenites, Kenizzites,
> Kadmonites, Hittites, Perizzites, Rephaim, Amorites, Canaanites,
> Girgashites, Jebusites."

And we continue, Genesis 17:5–14:

> "What's more," God told him, "I am changing your name. It is no
> longer Abram ('Exalted Father'), but Abraham ('Father of Nations')—
> for that is what you will be. I have declared it. I will give you millions
> of descendants who will be from many nations. Kings shall be among
> your descendants! And I will continue this agreement between us gen-
> eration after generation, forever, for it shall be between me and your
> children as well. It is a contract that I shall be your God and the God of
> your posterity. And I will give all this land of Canaan to you and them,
> forever. And I will be your God.
> "Your part of the contract," God told him, "is to obey its terms.
> You personally and all your posterity have this continual responsibility:
> that every male among you shall be circumcised; the foreskin of his
> penis shall be cut off. This will be the proof that you and they accept
> this covenant. Every male shall be circumcised on the eighth day after
> birth. This applies to every foreign-born slave as well as to everyone
> born in your household. This is a permanent part of this contract, and
> it applies to all your posterity. All must be circumcised. Your bodies
> will thus be marked as participants in my everlasting covenant. Anyone

who refuses these terms shall be cut off from his people; for he has violated my contract."

A strong statement, indeed. A metaphor with both Chosen People and Promised Land in it, a metaphor that has served as an archetype not only for Judaism but also for Christianity and Islam, in other words for the three semitic religions that together may be said to define the Occident. This First Covenant with Abraham is crystal clear, especially if we accept the interpretation of Wadi-el-Arish as the Nile.[1] And the First Covenant is then confirmed in the Second Covenant, with Moses on Mt. Sinai, set down in Exodus for everybody to read.[2]

A myth, some might say. And I would say it is the kind of raw material out of which history is made. The reality of this myth is proven by its tenacity, close to 4,000 years by now.

Let us then look at the other side. Professor Ismail Zayid of Dalhousie University in Halifax, Nova Scotia, Canada, writes in *The Guardian Weekly:*[3]

> Zionist re-writing of the history of Palestine is not a novelty, but your correspondents compound falsification with absurdity. Credible historians, including Arnold Toynbee, assert that the Palestinian Arabs of today are the descendants of the cumulative stock of the Canaanites, Philistines, Jebusites and others who inhabited Palestine, since the dawn of history and long before the Hebrew tribes invaded the Land of Canaan (Palestine).
>
> Professor Maxime Rodison of the Sorbonne in Paris, and himself Jewish, states: "The Arab population of Palestine was native in all the senses of the word and their roots in Palestine can be traced back at least forty centuries." H. G. Wells wrote, sixty years ago: "If it is proper to 'reconstitute' a Jewish state (in Palestine), which has not existed for two thousand years, why not go back another thousand years and reconstitute the Canaanite state? The Canaanites, unlike the Jews, are still there."

The reader will notice that there is some overlap between the nations mentioned in that particular area of the world: the Canaanites, the Jebusites. And Philistines = Palestinians.

Is it possible to know such things? I do not think that is even the correct question, not knowing the correct answer. Even if it is a myth, this is the kind of raw material out of which history is made. Whether the evidence presented can stand up to tests of modern historiography may be less important. The important point is an intense feeling of belongingness, of *homeland.*

Four thousand years of human history. This is a long span of time, and if there is one thing I have learned myself by working for twenty-five years now, off and on, as a peace researcher on this extremely complicated and intractable conflict, it is the following: the roots of the solution, if there are any, are found in the future, not in the past. It is my experience that it is not in any way helpful to try to survey these 4,000 years in order to score points as to who did more injustice to whom, who lived longest, where, in the largest numbers, and so on. Rather, I will extract three simple axioms from the past, and let them guide my search for a possible solution in the future. After having done that I will more or less say good-bye to the past, and invite everybody to share with me these visions, not so much different from visions many others might have, in the search for a viable future in the Middle-East.

Axiom 1: *The right to live in that area is an inalienable right both for Arabs and for Jews.* In other words, I take both justifications as quoted above not only as sufficient evidence for that inalienable right, but also as equal evidence. And that leads me immediately to

Axiom 2: *No viable peace can be obtained in the area except by according equal rights and duties to Arabs and Jews.* In other words, any solution based on concepts of "undivided Israel" or "undivided Palestine" to the exclusion of Arabs and Jews, respectively, is doomed in advance, even if the exclusion does not mean expulsion, leaving alone extermination, but any type of secondary citizenship. No security would ever be found within any such form. Whatever kind of peace in the sense of "absence of violence" that can be obtained will be of only short duration and at the expense of tremendous levels of repression, probably also exploitation, and in most cases direct violence or threats of direct violence. In other words, the peace spoken about is only absence of overt violence, it is not "peace" in any real sense, and certainly not security. To mix two metaphors: the peace of the cemetery, on top of a volcano. That is, until an *intifadah* (shaking off), like the present uprising in the occupied territories, shatters the illusions of acquiescence with the occupation December 9, 1987.

To these axioms should then be added a third:

Axiom 3: *Axioms 1 and 2 do not pertain only to the structure of a peaceful and viable solution, but also to any process leading to a via-*

ble solution. In other words, any peace process is doomed to fail unless the two parties, here only described as "Arabs" and "Jews" (in alphabetical order), are accorded equal rights and duties in the process. Stated more succinctly and with a very clear address to the Camp David "peace process" (that never was one according to axiom 3): accords arrived at over the heads of one of the parties concerned cannot be part of a viable peace process, and will hardly lead to any viable peace structure.[4]

At this point let me be more specific. Let it first be said that the area I am thinking of is not much different from the area described in Genesis 15:18, with the interpretation mentioned, but somewhat smaller. I am thinking particularly of mandated Palestine administered by Britain after the First World War, until it was divided (by Churchill) in 1922 into Cis-Jordania (roughly equal to the area today controlled by Israel) and Trans-Jordania (roughly equal to the area today controlled by the Hashemite Kingdom of Jordan).

In that area, what I refer to as the "Middle East conflicts" are a complex web of three conflicts: (1) between Jews and Arabs over state formation in Israel/Palestine (roughly speaking the same as Cis-Jordania); (2) the conflict between the Jewish state and surrounding Arab states; and (3) the conflict over who shall be the conflict manager for the region—the United States, the two superpowers in conjunction, the United Nations, all three, or "none of the above." To this could then be added a fourth conflict between superpowers and possibly also other outside powers with special interests in the area.

However, at the nucleus of this complex we find the conflict between Arabs and Jews over state formation, in other words the conflict between Israelis and Palestinians over Israel/Palestine. Even if conflicts nos. 2 and 3 were adequately solved to the satisfaction of all the parties involved, the solution would hardly be viable unless conflict no. 1 was also solved. From that it does not follow that if conflict no. 1 is solved, conflicts nos. 2 and 3 will be solved automatically. But it does not seem unreasonable to claim that there is more clearly a causal flow in that direction than from nos. 2 and 3 to no. 1. The uprising has brought out this point very clearly, and even if the Israelis should manage to dampen, even extinguish, these heavy manifestations of the underlying conflict, the Israelis will clearly be living on borrowed time. After a lull a new eruption, then a new lull, a new eruption, and so on and on.

And then, what? The Israelis used to have five options in the area:

status quo with more or less local autonomy, annexation 1, annexation 2, expulsion, and Palestinian state formation. *Annexation 1* would mean inclusion of the occupied territories in Gaza and the West Bank, giving to the Palestinians status as first-class citizens (with the possible exception of ministerial ranks, access to classified defense information and defense production information, and such areas). *Annexation 2* would mean inclusion of the same territories, but giving to the Palestinians only some kind of secondary class citizenship (among other reasons because of the "demographic time bomb"), like living where they are but voting in Jordan. But with an ongoing *intifadah,* the status quo is untenable, hence annexation 2 seems to be out. And the spread of the Palestinian revolt to areas inside the green line seems to indicate that annexation 1 is also out, and not only for demographic reasons.

What is left then would be "expulsion" and "Palestinian state formation." Roughly speaking these are the two options available but (so far) not articulated openly by the major Israeli parties, the Likud bloc and the Labor Party. What looks like efforts to maintain *status quo* barely conceals this incompatibility. If any actor in the area is a house divided against itself it must be Israel. And the rift seems to deepen with the growth of the orthodox parties.

The expulsion scenario would evict Palestinians to an area farther away from land they rightfully regard as theirs—the occupied territories of Gaza and the West Bank (and the Golan Heights) with a possible capital in East Jerusalem, and territory inside the green line. The scenario is tempting, of course, from an "undivided Israel" point of view because it would transform what today is an intra-state conflict into a set of inter-state conflicts that can be handled according to the conventional rules of the Westphalia "international system," with balance of power, strategic studies, occasional wars, and so on. But from a Palestinian point of view any such "solution" is totally unacceptable. All of this is totally incompatible with axioms 1 and 2 above; not to mention the international reaction.

The Palestinian state formation scenario would then be the only viable option of the four mentioned, but that in itself does not say very much in a solution-poor conflict. The question is what *kind* of state or states in the area, not only what kind of borders, and to explore that theme in more depth let me return to the axioms.

The options indicated by the extremists in the Middle-East, "undivided Israel" and "undivided Palestine," can serve the useful

Figure 1. Solving the Middle East Conflict: Three Options

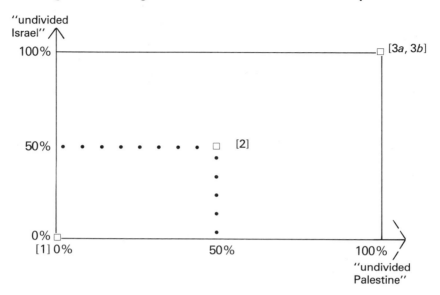

analytical purpose of identifying three other options, as indicated in Figure 1.

Option 1 is a 0–0 solution with neither the Arabs, nor the Jews, two nations, having any state in the area. Of course, this is what the Ottoman Empire was about, this is what the British Mandate was about, and today there are two clear successor possibilities within this first option. One possibility is a border zone, or for that matter the whole area, put under clearly defined United Nations peace-keeping control, abrogating the right not only of the Palestinians but also of the Israelis to have a state with ultimate control of violence inside the territory and monopoly on foreign policy, including the exercise of violence outside. It is also possible to imagine that the present U.S.-Soviet detente might reach a high point in a shared willingness to control, jointly, the whole area as a superpower condominium. In other words, it is fairly clear what option 1 would mean in practice in the near future. But taken alone it is a clear nonstarter.

Option 2 is a 50–50 solution, which would mean that both parties have the right to a state in the area. In other words, back to a partition plan. There would be an Israeli state, and also a Palestinian state, giving to the Palestinians the same rights as those given to the

Israelis of having a government, a parliament, a passport, and a flag. The Palestinian area would comprise all, or most, of the territories occupied in 1967, with a capital in East Jerusalem. In other words, "territories for peace"—as expressed repeatedly by the Arab side (Fez resolution 1987, Hussein-Arafat proposal 1985, Amman resolution 1987, and the agreement to give guarantees to all the states in the Middle East; culminating in the Algiers-Geneva-Stockholm resolutions late 1988). That 5 million Palestinians cannot make a living in that area is obvious. Nor can Israel house the total Jewish diaspora, but that is not an argument against the existence of Israel as a state with which Jews can identify.

It may certainly be objected that this solution was tried and failed in 1948. The Arab states around that central area attacked the new-born Israeli state. But before that the Jews had tried to seize as much of U.N.-allocated Arab Palestine as possible, including the massacre at Deir Yassin, 18 miles outside the borders allocated to a Jewish state before the British withdrawal (Plan Dalet). The argument could be that the same two scenarios might be enacted again.

Militarily, axiom 2 would, of course, rule out any effort to restrict forever the range of military weapons more severely in one of the states than in the other. Any such asymmetry is a way of communicating that one of the states is less trustworthy than the other. In other words, it is an asymmetric stigmatization, and unacceptable in any intense conflict for equal rights. If Israel does not like the idea of Palestine having any army at all, then the Palestinians might with equal justification say the same about Israel. If one of them is supposed to be disarmed, so also the other. If one of them is supposed to be transarmed, that is, possessing only means of defensive or nonprovocative defense, and no heavy weapons, so should the other. If one of them insists on a nuclear arsenal, so could the other. Again, the only viable lasting solution, including solution to the problem of security, is found in symmetry, and among those options defensive defense is by far the most stabilizing. However, detailed argumentation for this option lies outside the scope of this presentation. It should be noted that a Palestinian state would itself decide its relation to Jordan: open or latent enmity, coexistence, cooperation, confederation, federation, fusion. I do not see much basis for a prediction here, nor for knowing whether the last three possibilities would "Palestinize" Jordan or "Jordanize" Palestine.

Option 3 brings in a new element: the idea of transcending the conflict by bringing Arabs and Jews closer to each other (not Arabs and Arabs), on an equal basis, making "undivided Palestine" and "undivided Israel" compatible. Of course, total compatibility in the sense of the classical nation-state (one nation, one state) is impossible with (at least) two nations inhabiting the area. But there are at least two good possibilities within option 3: option 3a and option 3b.

Option 3a would bring in an additional element: a confederation, based on cantons, some Arab, some Jewish, in the area roughly corresponding to Cis-Jordania, or, better still, the whole area encompassed by the original mandate. A Swiss model, in other words, with open borders permitting the flow of persons, goods, services, and information inside,[5] but limiting, at least to start with, investment and settlement. If the Israelis could settle everywhere, they would be too strong economically and otherwise; if the Palestinians could settle everywhere, they would be too strong demographically (considering birth rates, and diaspora).

Since the confederation scenario is not often mentioned, let me be more specific. In such a scenario, there would be Arab cantons inside what today is known as Israel, for instance around Nazareth. There might also be Jewish cantons on the West Bank. In fact, one such canton might be exchanged for the other. Cantonization of all or parts of present Jordan (with at least 60% of the population being Palestinians) might be a part of the scenario. Cantons, and not necessarily only Palestinian, in present-day Sinai might be another part. Needless to say, all of this would depend on the ability of the actors in the area to convince each other and others that everybody would gain from a scheme of this kind. Jordan and Egypt might have to make some concessions.

Obviously, (all of) Jerusalem would be capital and federal territory, and the same principles would apply to Jerusalem as to the rest. The sum total of all the cantons would be known neither by the name of Israel nor by the name of Palestine, possibly by the two names hyphenated, possibly by a third name evocative of both or neither. There would certainly be a high level of internal government for the Arab cantons and for the Jewish cantons. But the sum total of Arab cantons would not be a Palestinian state in the sense defined above, nor would the sum total of Jewish cantons be identical with Israel of today or the successor state of Israel. But they would be sufficiently close for identification and cultural consistency. Palestinian law would apply in Arab cantons and Israeli law in Jewish cantons; disputes involving both would be settled by an overriding legal system. Neither would have a right to have an independent army. But the confederation as such might have an army for defense purposes, obviously with a defensive military doctrine.[6]

Option 3*b* is the image of the future often put forward by the Palestinian side, for instance by Al-Fatah: a secular state where Jews and Arabs (and Christians and others) live side by side. The area might roughly correspond to Cis-Jordania. In this vision there is an expression of the much higher ability of Moslems to accommodate Jews and Christians than vice versa. Islam has a concept of the religions of the *Kitab* (Old Testament); the other two exclude Islam with the concept of the Judeo-Christian faith. Catholic Spain (1492) evicted both Moslems and Jews; the Jews could settle for centuries in a number of Moslem countries (the "Oriental Jews") without being treated the way they were treated by Christians—Catholic, Protestant, Orthodox. Moreover, PLO was already an organization accommodating all three, together with secular Palestinians.

How about U.N membership? For the two-state solution of option 2 this is unproblematic: presumably both of them would be fully fledged U.N. members. For options 3*a* and 3*b* this is more problematic. Membership could be granted, but that newborn U.N. member might have considerable difficulties making up its mind. However, is it obvious that it would be so difficult? Could it not rather be that most of the agenda items for the General Assembly are of such a kind that what Jews and Arabs, Israelis and Palestinians in that Third World region have in common in terms of interests might quickly be more important than the things that divide them? Obviously there would be many items on the U.N. political agenda to which the adequate response would be either abstention or nonparticipation in the vote. But it is not a given in advance that this would be the case with the majority of items.

What kind of flag, what kind of national anthem, which holidays to celebrate, what kind of monetary unit (what would it look like, what would it be called) . . . ? Option 2 could creep into option 3*a* by answering these questions in terms of two flags, two anthems, separate holidays, separate coinage (as long as they are freely interchangeable). But sooner or later more imaginative solutions would come about. The coin, like the stamps, could be printed in both languages (possibly also in English). Symbols of one group likely to provoke the other would be ruled out. A search for joint symbols would take place. At some point or another a fascinating ecumenical dialogue might even take place, and in such a way that Christians are not excluded. They might even come to know each other and respect each other, with as many Jews talking Arabic as today there are Arabs talking Hebrew.

The obvious question now would be: Which one of these four options is best and should be preferred? And my answer would be: all four of them. I do not think we promote conflict resolution in the Middle East by thinking in mutually exclusive terms about the options on the main diagonal of Figure 1. The important point is to regard these four options as exhaustive, not as mutually exclusive. "Undivided Palestine" and "undivided Israel" are the options to be excluded as leading but to death, with more decades, generations, centuries of humiliation, exploitation, suppression, expulsion, extermination.

The four options on the main diagonal can be combined in many ways:

Thus, option 2 might be seen as a first stage toward option 3*a*. Option 3*b* might then be presented as an ultimate goal, for a future more likely to be remote than near. Given the enmity, even hatred, between the participants and the sharing of extremely bad experiences, not only during the last forty years but during the last 4,000, the idea of these participants running a state together at all levels, from the top to the smallest municipal unit, smacks of the utopian. Nevertheless, as a distant goal it might one day become interesting even if the Jews would be a minority in a secular state.

For the transition from option 2 to option 3*a*, a timetable should be given. Twenty years? Twenty-five? Forty—after a new generation has come to power in both states? Israel/Palestine would then be conceptualized as a divided country from the beginning, begging the question of unification. And, not unlike two other divided countries, Germany and Korea, total unification may sound utopian, but some type of confederate association would not. There are powerful similarities. And the difference: one divided nation, versus two nations.

It is important in this connection to emphasize that in option 3*a* there should be more than one Arab canton, and more than one Jewish canton. With only one of either kind we are essentially back to the two-state solution. Bipolarity is already built into the structure from the very beginning. With several Arab and several Jewish cantons, other alliance patterns might emerge, or at least a pattern of interaction among cantons different from what we would expect from pure ethnic bipolarity. In other words, the model would be Switzerland rather than Belgium as it is often conceptualized, one part Flemish and the other part Walloon, with Brussels in between. Of course, there is a concept of German Switzerland and French Switzerland, the two most important parts of Switzerland. But the bipolarity is mellowed by the presence of a third party (Swizzera Italiana, and even a fourth, the Rheto-Roman), and the multiplicity of cantons of either kind.

Option 1 enters as a guarantee, to be brought into the peace process at an early stage and then gradually lifted. One could think in terms of U.N. peace-keeping forces for the Israel/Palestine conflict and superpower guarantees for the Israel/Arab states conflict. In that way all candidates for positions as ultimate conflict managers would get some say. None of them, however, would be in a position to dictate the final solution. At the same time it would be more difficult for Israelis and Palestinians to continue fighting, and for Israel and Arab states to launch one more war in their succession of wars 1948, 1956, 1967, 1973, 1982—one per decade? Is the next due in the early 1990s, barring the creation of some new political geography?

In short, a viable peace plan based on symmetry would also have a built-in process by which all four options could be brought into the picture. And that brings us to axiom 3: the application of the same type of ideas to the peace process itself.

Of course, a comprehensive and lasting international conference is needed for the articulation of all the interests in the area (and they are many). The conference should be convened and organized by the United Nations which for that purpose might consider adding a new specialized organ to the family of U.N. organizations. Both superpowers would participate, and equally. If one superpower is afraid the other might make use of the conference for "propaganda purposes," there are two clear solutions to that problem: to call the propaganda a bluff, or, if there is some reality to it, to change that reality, thereby demolishing the propaganda.

Obviously both Israelis and Palestinians would belong as fully fledged members. How many other countries would be invited to participate, and with what status, should probably be up to the two superpowers and the two major conflict actors, in conjunction with the U.N. officials, to decide. Obviously "all states in the area" would be invited; the problem is how to define the "area."

No asymmetry should be tolerated in connection with the composition of the delegations. Any idea to the effect that one party should not be empowered to select its own delegation is a way of communicating second-class legitimacy. There can be no other basis than complete symmetry for a peace process to be successful in this field of tension. If one party insists on weeding out members in the delegation of the other side, for instance because of participation in "terrorism," so could the other party. If one party insists on freely electing and selecting the members of its own delegation, so will the other party. And within the symmetrical options, self-determination for all parties seems by far to be the most viable option. Incidentally, this would in all probability lead to the presence of a certain number of past and present terrorists in all delegations. Such is the century we inhabit. A terrorist-free conference room will be nearly empty.

How much time would a conference of this type need in order to produce a viable outcome? Nobody knows. But we are talking about years rather than months. If they got started today they might be finished before the mid-1990s. If they had started six years ago (at the time of the Fez resolution of September 1982) we might have had a much better state of affairs in the area than we have today. Of course, any such solution would essentially have to be made according to the "territories for peace" formula: Israel would give up monopolistic control over some parts of the total territory; Palestine would get some. Israel would gain in security, meaning peace without Palestine losing security; they had none. And then, according to options 3*a* and 3*b*, it is not obvious that the Israelis would lose access to territory. We would assume that some Israelis would live in Palestinian cantons and vice versa, much as French-speaking people can be found in German cantons in Switzerland and vice versa. There might be restrictions on property rights and permanent settlement, however.

Let us now compare this vision with other images of a stable and lasting peace in the Middle East. I shall start with a fairly extensive quote from "A Blueprint for Peace," taken from the *Jerusalem Post*,[7] by Shlomo Maoz who writes it as a government communique after "an all night debate on the future of the Gaza Strip":

Israel is to leave the Gaza Strip at midnight on Sunday, December 31, 1989. The Israeli government is ready to deal with any representatives of the Arab world to coordinate Israel's withdrawal. If no representative can be found to enable a swift transfer, Israel will withdraw unilaterally.

Israel will not interfere with the newborn state in any way. However, if heavy weapons are introduced, Israel has the right and the power to take action. For this reason, Israel will retain its right to use certain advanced devices for the purpose of keeping a check on potential threats from the newly independent area.

Israel is ready to assist the newly independent state by granting $1 billion over a five-year period. At the same time, Israel will look for additional international help to establish a viable economy.

The Gazans will be encouraged by Israel to develop a deep-water port that will be used in a free-trade zone and for the hinterland, which includes the West Bank, Jordan, and the Gulf countries. Israel will provide an open corridor from the Strip to the West Bank or to Jordan River bridges. The new port will be designated for commercial vessels only and will not be used by naval craft. . . .

Israel will provide alternative access to the Red Sea through a new road along the Egyptian border, which will allow trade and transportation between the Strip and Aqaba (and Elat) and Saudi Arabia.

If the Gazans choose to continue the trade in goods and services with Israel, including sending workers to Israel, this trade will go through two checkpoints, where inhabitants of each side will require permits to enter the other's domain.

Economic relations between the two countries will be determined through a bilateral agreement. Israel hopes that there will be a free-trade zone between the two countries. In that case, Gaza, with its new port and possibly an international airport for passenger and commercial traffic, will be able to compete with Israel.

Israel will keep the relationship with the Gaza Strip under constant review, hoping to regard its progress during the first decade as a basis for negotiations over the future of the West Bank.

As Maoz points out we are talking here about 600,000 people who are supposed to make a living from the 140 square miles of the Gaza Strip. His idea, shared by many, is that Gaza should become the Singapore of the Middle East. "With no military expenditures, all their efforts would go into economic development." He envisions prosperity not only for the Gazans but also for the region, while Israel not only would get peace relative to the people of the Gaza Strip, but also would have 600,000 fewer Arab inhabitants, so the "demographic bomb" would be partially neutralized. And he goes on making a very important point which can be substantiated by looking at the history of the Roman Empire. Precisely because Israel has access to cheap labor (using the "slave market" method, of Palestinians from Gaza coming in by bus early in the morning to Jerusalem searching for menial and underpaid jobs), there is no incentive to develop a higher level of technology. In other words, Israel would be forced to become more competitive. And it might become less of the subsidized, essentially Third World country, it is today.

Some points are missing from the plan and could easily be added:

For one thing, why should it apply only to the Gaza Strip? If Israel provides an open corridor from the Strip to the West Bank, then that open corridor could also unite these two parts of a Palestinian state and include a capital in East Jerusalem. The West Bank is not densely populated; Gaza is. The viability of Gaza alone is to be doubted; the viability of the two together can be discussed. Of course, that viability would be greatly increased with the type of addition mentioned above, which might also be in the interest of Jordan and Egypt if they want to retain peace in the area. But, of course, the West Bank is theologically much more sensitive (Judea, Sumaria).

Second, the British withdrew unilaterally in 1948 without leaving —which at that time would have been impossible—some kind of U.N. peace-keeping force behind. It would hardly be a good idea for Israel to repeat this mistake. Two things might happen: Egypt might move in to occupy Gaza, and/or Israeli elements might move to occupy what they consider theirs. To what extent the latter would then be on a collision course with their own government remains to be seen. It is hard to believe that within the foreseeable future the basic division of interests and values within Israel, from the bottom up to the very top of society, as represented by alternating prime ministers, will be healed. Something corresponding to Plan Dalet might still be enacted.

What is so imaginative about the scenario is the vision of a high-status economy for Gaza; not the continuation of dominance by other means by relegating the Palestinians forever to inferior roles in the international division of labor. In short, except for the two points made, this is a blueprint that tastes of realism, not of the idealism (in the sense of being removed from reality) of the current Israeli head of government who, as Moaz points out, "believes that he himself can represent [the Palestinians]."

This could then be compared to the six-point plan suggested at the time by a U.S. foreign minister as an example of a different way of thinking. One presentation of the plan[8] with its six points runs as follows:

1. After a six-month transition period, Jordanian or international troops shall replace Israeli troops in the occupied territories.

2. Afterward, the Palestinians can choose their own representative, who will be responsible for all nonmilitary functions.

3. Under international auspices an Israeli-Arab dialogue will be initiated.

4. The PLO representative can send his confidants (however, no PLO activists) to these negotiations in a combined Jordanian-Palestinian delegation.

5. At the end of this (at the most, three-year planned) dialogue begins the evacuation of the over-twenty-years occupied territories—with "small, cosmetic border changes."

6. The final status of Jerusalem remains, for the time being, undecided. However, in any case, the Arab inhabitants of the East Quarter must have the right to choose their own representative.

Many factors combine to make this a very unrealistic blueprint for a stable and enduring peace, including when it was discussed in 1987/88.

First, there is the U.S. obsession with Jordan. One might have believed that after the experience with Iran and the Shah, Washington would have developed a higher level of sophistication in understanding how nonviable such regimes, so far removed from their own population, tend to be. A country like Jordan, with at least 60% Palestinians and the fresh memory in the minds of all of them of Black September, does not give to the Jordan government much latitude. Moreover, King Hussein himself has repeatedly rejected "the Jordanian option" (and then, in July 1988, eliminated it).

On the other hand, there is a mention of "international troops." But that term is in itself ambiguous. It might stand for the U.N. peace-keeping force, but also for a multinational force of the type that the United States launched (together with Britain, France, and Italy) in Lebanon in 1983. The United States part ended with the death of 241 U.S. marines. And the United States still has to understand that, however critical the country is of the United Nations, that organization nevertheless bestows more legitimacy on "international troops" than on any multilateral force put together by the United States and her allies, in Lebanon, the Gulf, or elsewhere.

Second, the Palestinians have to choose their own representative from the very beginning. The point made in axiom 3 above is that the process has to be similar (or at least not too dissimilar) to the end result for the whole solution to stick. The U.S. plan rejects this.

Third, there is again the ambiguity of "international auspices." If it means a United Nations setting, there is no problem. If it means a U.S.-monitored and choreographed conference, then there is. And this should not be point 3 chronologically in any case. This should be point 1, starting immediately. Moreover, it might be pointed out that there are two dialogues or a trilateral dialogue involved: an Israeli/Palestinian dialogue and an Israel/Arab states dialogue. The former is outlawed in Israel.[9] There is not one "Israel/Arab" conflict, as the discourse runs in Israel, in the effort to make Palestinians invisible.

Fourth, again there is the obsession with Jordan. The comment most adequate to this point would be "nonsense"—because it is based on a fiction. The word *activist* is probably a synonym for *terrorist*. In either case there is a problem. The *intifadah* revolt has probably made most Palestinians, not to mention most PLO adherents (and that means most Palestinians), PLO activists anyhow, meaning that there would not be much to choose from. But if the line is drawn at the "terrorist" point, a number of people would also have to be excluded from the Israeli side, including the prime minister himself. As urged repeatedly above: let each party select its own representatives and do not try to interfere with the selections of the others. Admittedly there are some cases where some persons may be particularly provocative in negotiations. But it is not obvious that those persons are found more among the Palestinians than among, for instance, the Israelis and the Americans. Again, let symmetry be the guide.

Fifth, a very positive point about this plan is that it talks about "occupied territories" in plural. In other words, in principle all four could be included in the plan, meaning also East Jerusalem and the Golan Heights. However, this is not the United States' intention since Jerusalem will not again be partitioned.

Sixth, and this is the point about Jerusalem: it is unimaginative and will probably satisfy nobody.

More important, however, is the point not stated among the six: no independent Palestinian state would be established. And this makes the whole plan simply hang in the air. If Jordanian troops are to do the supervision, then this would mean an expansion of the Hashemite kingdom of Jordan. However impressed Washington may be with Black September, that is hardly a precedent for the future. Just to the contrary: the obvious outcome of a plan like this would be an immediate revolt by Palestinians, after the "supervision" by Jordanian troops even more in a majority than ever before.

In short, this is a plan with very serious political deficits, to some extent derived from short-term Israeli and U.S. interests, but also indicative of equally serious intellectual deficits. The only positive point is the idea of negotiation; but then the plan should be limited to that point alone, without dictating the outcome. In general, recognition of the other party should be an outcome of a conference, not a precondition couched in terms that makes it a nonstarter.

Let me now return to the general theory of peace and conflict resolution and try to retrace the thinking that has been presented above, adding new elements in a more complete scenario. In order to do so I shall use the six-fold approach to conflict resolution based on the *A, B, C* triangle (of attitudes, behavior, and conflict) and the intra-, inter-distinction for any conflict. One should then keep in mind that no linear approach to these six points is assumed. We cannot start with just one of these points hoping that the other five will follow in its wake by some kind of domino effect. Rather, all six have to be approached as nearly simultaneously as possible, not saying by that that some points are not more important than the others. But they are important in terms of the consequences if nothing is done, not as causal levers for all the other points.

Thus clear, powerful visions of the future of the whole area have to emerge. Let one thousand blueprints flourish. Let there be dialogues all over the place. Organize conferences of those with blueprints. I would, of course, stand by the three axioms announced in the beginning of this presentation. But they are so generally formulated as to be compatible with a variety of different scenarios.

On the other hand, the axioms certainly focus the attention on the main diagonal of Figure 1. And along that diagonal four options have been indicated. All four can be spelled out in more detail. Thus, in connection with option *3a* the point can certainly be made that the area is not yet ready for cantonization. But is that really the case? Is it not rather the case that we know fairly well where some Jewish cantons would be and where some Arab cantons would be, and that the controversy would be over a third category, ambiguous areas contested by both parties? So, why not operate with a division in three parts and accord some special status to the third category, at least to start with? "Gray" cantons, their position to be decided later?

However, more imagination should be put into the "meta-option" of combining the four options. This can be done along a time scale, as mentioned, starting in the bottom left-hand corner of Figure 1 and working upward. But as the process proceeds options 1 and 2 will gradually be left behind in favor of options $3a$ and $3b$. In other words, some kind of peace can be obtained at a relatively early stage of the process; a more stable and enduring peace only at the later stages, as most people would agree—a progression from peace-keeping to peace-making to peace-building.

If we now switch from the focus on the inter-aspects to the intra-aspects, there is no doubt that conflict resolution requires considerable conflict management inside Israel, including the relationship of the country to the United States; and inside Palestine, including the relation of the Palestinians to other Arab states. (I do not see the Soviet Union having a relation to Palestine in any way similar to the relation the United States has to Israel. Of course, there are some similarities between the relationship the Soviet Union has to Syria and the United States to Egypt, not to mention to Saudi Arabia, but that is another matter.) In general this corner of the six-fold scheme would probably be more a question of patient persuasion, Israelis and Palestinians alike persuading other Israelis and Palestinians that the conference outcome might be the best solution.

Turning now to behavioral inter-relations: the best thing Israel could do would be to help the new Palestinian state develop so that later on it could easily enter a confederation. Few things should be so meaningful in international relations as the imprinting of a newborn state with acts of generosity, for instance along the line suggested by the excellent *Jerusalem Post* article quoted above. An objection might be that it is easy to be generous with somebody else's money. A billion dollars per year—while the United States subsidizes Israel to the tune of 3 to 4 billion dollars a year, assuming that the whole plan would also make the defense burden easier to carry for the Israelis— might be less generous than it sounds. And yet the spirit is important —concrete, positive acts. It would not be in Israel's interest that all the support for a new Palestinian state should come from the Arab side, nor from the Palestinian community in diaspora.

The intra-aspect corresponding to this would be transarmament of Israel, meaning disarmament of particularly offensive systems, including the nuclear capability. It is difficult to see how this could be done without putting similar demands on Iraq and Pakistan (with its "Islamic" bomb). Deep international inspection by the appropriate U.N. organization (IAEA) would be indispensable. On the other hand, it could also be argued that this problem is so touchy that it should be left for later stages. The process might have to prove itself before the most offensive weapons are touched (after all, this may be what is now happening in the East-West conflict). Evidently, the more successful the process the more will these weapons recede into the background, unless we assume completely genocidal (or suicidal) inclinations on either side.

Finally, then, we come to the basic question of attitudes. We enter the field of perceptions of Self and perceptions of Other—on both sides. More particularly, we enter the field of the relation between these two perceptions, the two "Self-Other gradients." If the Self-perception is very enhanced and the Other-perception is very debased, dehumanized, then the Self-Other gradient is pathological. Something has to be done. It has to be repaired, even across the distance of decades, generations, centuries, millennia, to attain more normal human proportions. The word *ethnocentricity* covers this very badly. The point is not only a certain centeredness on Self and some Self enhancement above what others might accord to that person or people. Faith in oneSelf may be seen as normal and natural, perhaps even as positive. The dangerous point comes when in addition Other is dehumanized making the Self-Other gradient so steep that almost any amount of structural violence (exploitation, repression) and even direct violence (expulsion, extermination) become totally normal and natural consequences of the images held.

Since that steep gradient is so deeply entrenched in the exponents of hard Judaism (whom I prefer not to quote) we have to turn to a master of soft Judaism, Martin Buber, for inspiration. For him the demand for a Jewish state with a Jewish majority was of less importance:[10]

> We need for this land as many Jews as it is possible economically to absorb, but not in order to establish a majority against a minority. We

need them because great, very great forces are required to do the
unprecedented work. We need for this land a solid, vigorous, autonomous community, but not in order that it should give its name to a
state; we need it because we want to raise Israel and *Eretz Israel* to the
highest level of productivity they can be raised to. The new situation
and the problem involved ask for new solutions that are beyond the
capacity of the familiar political categories. An internationally guaranteed agreement between the two communities is asked for, which
defines the spheres of interest and activity common to the partners and
those not common to them, and guarantees mutual non-interference
for these specific spheres.

Notice the words "the two communities"—very compatible with
the confederation idea; less with the two-states idea and also less with
the single-state idea. Buber refers to the creativity, indeed to the
potential inherent in any people and seems to want it to grow, but
not at the expense of any other people. "The highest level of productivity" is certainly meant not only in economic terms. It is a very powerful vision; "a zionism of quality, not acres" (Harkabi).

But it does presuppose some deconstruction of the basic Jewish
myth with which this presentation was started. Nobody will rewrite
Genesis and Exodus (although this has certainly been done in the
past), or the whole Torah for that matter. But it certainly would help
if very many Jews, maybe the majority, could see this as a tale to be
celebrated on the appropriate occasions, not as a blueprint for geopolitical expansionism. The eminently justifiable pride in Jewish
achievements and contributions to world culture, and the horror of
the barbarism to which Jews have been exposed should be delinked
from geopolitical expansionism. There will be no "greater Israel."

And, finally, is this plan realistic? In the sense of being immediately acceptable to all parties included, certainly not. In the sense of
being at least as realistic as other plans, certainly yes. The three conflicts are simply intractable; a "situation" (to use very noninflamma-
tory U.N. language) for which the British with their tendency to
move people (in South Africa, East Africa, Trinidad, Fiji, Falkland/
Malvinas, Gibraltar, Ulster, to mention some places) will have to take
much of the blame. But they are not totally beyond solution.

We cannot stay with these conflicts forever. History has to move
on. And the experience is rather unambiguous: only an equitable
solution is a viable solution.

*   *   *

Please note:

After this lecture was given, in the spring of 1988, King Hussein renounced any rights on Jordan, thereby eliminating "the Jordanian option" (except as a part of a federation later on); the PNC declared the Palestinian state on November 15, 1988, and the *initfadah* continued, undaunted by the efforts to suppress it. Although there is still a long distance to go, the process has been moved significantly in the direction advocated in this chapter.

NOTES

CHAPTER I

1. A little anecdote. In June 1962 I was invited to a conference organized by Kwame Nkrumah, the *osagyefoh* (savior) of Ghana, "The World Without a Bomb," in Accra. The spokesmen for the superpowers (the Soviet representative later on became deputy foreign minister of his country, the U.S. representative was a less prominent arms control negotiator) laid out their positions. Next to me was a Ghanaian chief with a leopard skin nicely draped over the shoulder. He asked me: "Is that the Soviet man? Is that the U.S. man? Is what they talk about that Cold War we hear so much about? Is that really all? And they cannot solve that one? . . . In my place we just sit down and talk till we are through with it."

2. According to Associate Astronomer Charles Lindsey of the University of Hawaii, in a letter of April 15, 1988. The AVCO research is classified, the Lunar Ranging Experiment (LURE) carried out by the University of Hawaii at the same place "is purely scientific, is completely open and has no relation to the Defense Department or SDI."

3. See the article by Mikhail Gorbachev, "The Realities and Guarantees of a Secure World," *Pravda,* September 17, 1987. For a discussion in nonofficial United States, see Mark Sommer, *An Emerging Consensus: Common Security Through Qualitative Disarmament,* Alternative Defense Project, The Fund for Peace, New York, 1988.

4. For an effort to discuss the East-West conflict in a more wholistic manner, see my *Europe in the Making* (New York: Taylor & Francis, 1989).

5. For a development of this theme, see my "The Cold War as an Exercise in Autism: The U.S. Government, the Governments of Western Europe—and the People," *Essays in Peace Research,* vol. VI (Copenhagen: Ejlers, 1988), chapter 5.

6. The International Bill of Human Rights consists of the Universal Declaration of Human Rights; the International Covenant on Economic, Social, and Cultural Rights; the International Covenant on Civil and Political Rights; and the Optional Protocol on Civil and Political Rights.

7. For a comparison between the Atlantic and the Pacific theaters of the Cold War, see chapter 2 in my *Peace and Development In the Pacific Hemisphere* (Honolulu: University of Hawaii Press, 1989).

8. For a development of this theme, see my "The European Community: A Superpower in the Making?", chapter 11 in *Essays in Peace Research,* vol. VI.

9. The most important is SPD in Germany, which in its program from June 1986 states that NATO should be *strikt defensiv* and talks about *Abbau von Drohpotentialen bis hin zur beiderseitigen strukturellen Nichtangriffsfähigkeit.*

10. The most important is the Labour Party in Britain which states very clearly that the reliance on nuclear weapons must be brought to an end and that NATO's conventional strength must be enhanced.

11. For many details about this kind of combination, see my *There Are Alternatives* (Nottingham: Spokesman, 1984), chapter 5.

12. The only detailed, publicly available, work in this direction to my knowledge is by David Fish, a Ph.D. candidate at the University of Hawaii Department of Political Science, to be published by the *Journal of Peace Research* in 1989.

13. Carl Sagan, "The Common Enemy," *Parade Magazine,* Honolulu, February 7, 1988.

14. Under the current *glasnost'* conditions, the teaching of history in the Soviet Union has certainly become a major issue. But U.S. (and in general Western) history books may also be in need of revision, and one wonders under what conditions such revisions would be initiated.

15. For an exploration of U.S. fantasies in this direction, see my *United States Foreign Policy as Manifest Theology,* University of California, San Diego, Institute on Global Conflict and Cooperation, IGCC Policy Paper no. 4, 1987. For a comparison of the two fantasies entertained by the two superpowers, see chapter 3 in *Europe in the Making,* "U.S. and Soviet World Myths: Contradictory or Compatible?"

CHAPTER 2

1. See my "A Structural Theory of Imperialism," *Essays in Peace Research,* vol. IV (Copenhagen: Ejlers, 1980), chapter 13; and " 'A Structural Theory of Imperialism'–10 Years Later," *Essays in Peace Research,* vol. VI (1988), chapter 17.

2. A very important argument from a seller's point of view. But the public opinion poll taken in Hawaii on this issue was very clear: 78% against foreign home buyers for investment (as against only 38% against if foreigners buy homes to live in), *Honolulu Advertiser,* May 15, 1988.

3. A term unfortunately missing from most U.S. economic and political discourse, making it very difficult to clarify issues. The term is often seen as contentious, controversial—presumably because it refers to a highly contentious and controversial reality. There are those who enjoy exploitation more than others, just as there were those who enjoyed slave trading more than did others.

4. The $1 = Yen 360 looked like a law of nature till 1971. From then on the decline has been clear although with ups and downs. $1 = Yen 100 is in sight. Not much knowledge of the world economy was necessary to predict that decline.

5. *Honolulu Advertiser,* to be precise. "The Japanese are doing to us with cash what they were not able to do with bullets and bombs, taking over our state," said one of the demonstrators.

6. According to the *Honolulu Advertiser,* August 8, 1987, high school students in

Japan were polled about the chances that Japan will again wage war. Most thought not (62%), and the 38% who thought yes were then asked about the likely adversary. "49 percent picked the United States as Japan's likely adversary, compared with 41 percent for the Soviet Union and 3 percent for China." In other words, 90:3 Occident:Orient, which tells something about Japanese readings of the world. And then it becomes painfully clear how unrealistic Washington is in its assumptions about how Japanese youth see the two superpowers; 41:49 is very far from the 100:0 Washington might have liked to see.

7. See Johan Galtung, Peter O'Brien, and Adrian Preiswerk, *Self-Reliance* (London: Bougle-d'Ouverture, 1980).

8. See my "On the Dialectic Between Crisis and Crisis Perception," *International Journal of Comparative Sociology* 25, nos. 1–2 (1984).

9. It is the theme throughout his important *Turning the Tide* (Boston: South End Press, 1986).

10. See my *United States Foreign Policy as Manifest Theology,* University of California, San Diego, IGCC Policy Papers no. 4, 1987.

11. See my *Glasnost' U.S.A.,* Ablex Publishing Corporation, Norwood N.J., forthcoming, for an exploration of this rather comprehensive theme.

12. Japan's foreign economic policy does not fulfill this criterion better than U.S. policy. The unknown theoretician behind the Japanese "economic miracle" and the "Flying Geese" theory, Akamatsu Kaname, had in mind to make Japan rich, not to promote peace (see the article by, in a sense his pupil, Okita Saburo, "Japan, China and the United States: Economic Relations and Prospects," *Foreign Affairs,* Summer 1979, pp. 1090–1110).

CHAPTER 3

1. However, in Numbers 34 very concrete borders are given. And Numbers 33:50–56 give an almost exact formula for present-day Israeli policies: "You must drive out all the people living there and destroy all their idols." "You will be given land in proportion to the size of your tribes." "If you refuse to drive out the people living there, those who remain will be as cinders in your eyes and thorns in your sides. And I will destroy you as I had planned for you to destroy them."

2. Whereas the First Covenant is more geopolitical, the Second Covenant is more moral—with the Ten Commandments, for instance.

3. March 13, 1988. Also see Genesis 10:15–18.

4. For an analysis of this from a moderate Arab point of view, see Fayez A. Sayegh, Senior Consultant, Ministry of Foreign Affairs, Kuwait, *Camp David and Palestine; A Preliminary Analysis,* New York, October 1978.

5. Inside Israel, and in the world at large, Joseph Abileah, former concert master of the Haifa Symphony Orchestra, has very actively promoted the confederation idea. For an early presentation of my own version, see "The Middle East and the Theory of Conflict," *Essays in Peace Research,* vol. V (Copenhagen: Ejlers, 1980), pp. 77ff. (originally published in the *Journal of Peace Research,* 1971.)

6. See my *There Are Alternatives* (Nottingham: Spokesman, 1984), chapter 5, for some details about how and why this type of defense is particularly compatible with

confederate decentralization. Is it to be ruled out completely that one day Israelis and Palestinians might have a joint interest in defending their joint country against attacks from neighboring states? In other words, a joint IDF-PLO force against attacks from anybody?

7. As excerpted by the *World Press Review,* December 1987.

8. The Schultz plan probably has some flexibility in it, so formulations should not be taken too literally.

9. The law passed in August 1986 by the Knesset prohibits any contacts between Israel and PLO activists, making meetings that had been going on for years illegal. However, just as in the DDR and in the Soviet Union, Israeli scholars can participate in academic conferences even when persons affiliated with the PLO are present, provided such conferences are held by an academic institute and the subject of the conference is academic.

10. Quoted from M. H. Ellis, *Towards a Jewish Theology of Liberation* (New York City: Orbis, Maryknoll, 1987).

DATE DUE

MY 03 '02			
OC 27 03			

DEMCO 38-297